THE FIRST BATTLES

A SOURCEBOOK ON THE CIVIL WAR

THE FIRST
BATTLES

A SOURCEBOOK ON THE CIVIL WAR

Edited by Carter Smith

AMERICAN ALBUMS FROM THE COLLECTIONS OF
THE LIBRARY OF CONGRESS

THE MILLBROOK PRESS, *Brookfield, Connecticut*

Cover: "The Battle of Shiloh, or Pittsburg Landing." Music cover by Charles Grobe, 1862.

Title Page: "Camp Davies." Lithograph by Rosenthal, 1862.

Contents Page: "Off for the War." Lithograph by Currier & Ives, 1861.

Back Cover: "The Battle between the Monitor and the Merrimack." Lithograph by Kurz & Allison, nineteenth century.

Library of Congress Cataloging-in-Publication Data

The First battles : a sourcebook on the Civil War / edited by Carter Smith.
     p. cm. — (American albums from the collections of the Library of Congress)
    Includes bibliographical references and index.
    Summary: Uses a variety of contemporary materials to describe and illustrate the early battles in the Civil War from the firing on Fort Sumter in April 1861 to the conflict at Fredericksburg at the end of 1862.
    ISBN 1-56294-262-X (lib. bdg.)
    1. United States—History—Civil War, 1861–1865—Campaigns—Juvenile literature. 2. United States—History—Civil War, 1861–1865—Campaigns—Pictorial works—Juvenile literature. 3. United States—History—Civil War, 1861–1865—Campaigns—Sources—Juvenile literature. [1. United States—History—Civil War, 1861–1865—Campaigns—Sources.] I. Smith, C. Carter. II. Series.
E470.F55 1993
973.7'31'0222—dc20

                                    92-16544
                                          CIP
                                          AC

 Created in association with Media Projects Incorporated

C. Carter Smith, *Executive Editor*
Lelia Wardwell, *Managing Editor*
Charles A. Wills, *Principal Writer*
Kimberly Horstman, *Picture and Production Editor*
Lydia Link, *Designer*
Athena Angelos, *Photo Researcher*

The consultation of Bernard F. Reilly, Jr., Head Curator of the Prints and Photographs Division of the Library of Congress, is gratefully acknowledged.

10 9 8 7 6 5 4 3 2 1

256 80142

Contents

The events of the Civil War inspired hundreds of songs in both the Union and the Confederacy. Shown here is the sheet-music cover to a "grand march," dedicated to the "Shepard Rifles," a volunteer regiment from New York. One Civil War song, "When This Cruel War is Over," sold a million copies in sheet-music form.

Introduction

THE FIRST BATTLES is one of the volumes in a series published by The Millbrook Press titled AMERICAN ALBUMS FROM THE COLLECTIONS OF THE LIBRARY OF CONGRESS, and one of six books in the series subtitled SOURCEBOOKS ON THE CIVIL WAR.

The editors' basic goal for the series is to make available to the student many of the original visual documents preserved in the Library of Congress as records of the American past. The volumes in THE CIVIL WAR series reproduce many of the prints, broadsides, maps, and other works kept in the Library's special collections divisions, and a few from its general book collections. The series features prominently the holdings of the Prints and Photographs Division.

The great national trauma of the American Civil War generated an extraordinary number and variety of images. The initial flood of Northern patriotism precipitated by the Confederate attack on Fort Sumter produced thousands of pictures, such as illustrations on common objects like sheet-music covers and tobacco labels, as well as highly romanticized (and highly inaccurate) views of early Union victories.

More objective and reliable as records of the war are the works of field artists and photographers. Several artists employed as reporters for major New York newspapers captured in their drawings a vital record of the character and progress of the war. Alfred Waud's on-the-spot drawings of the flight of Union troops at the Second Battle of Bull Run and the Union landing at Hampton Roads are extremely important and telling documents of their time. On the other hand, the photographs taken during the war possess admirable detail and enviable factuality, but for technical reasons were limited to subjects that would stand still, largely portraits and landscapes. In their day, the photographs of Alexander Gardner, George Barnard, and others nonetheless shocked the American public with the magnitude of death and destruction wrought by the armies of North and South.

It is worth noting that much of the visual record of the war was the product of Northern reporting. Most images of the Southern war effort date from after the war. This was because by 1861 the major media of the period—photography and lithography—were as yet little developed in the South.

The works reproduced here represent a small portion of the rich pictorial record of the Civil War, preserved by the Library of Congress in its role as the nation's library.

BERNARD F. REILLY, JR.

The United States split into two separate nations, the Union and the Confederacy, in 1861. As this map shows, geography as well as slavery formed the dividing lines between the two nations. But while the lines are fixed on this map, they were less clear in the minds of many Americans.

By the First Battle of Bull Run in July 1861, the Confederacy comprised eleven slave-holding states. But four slave states—Delaware, Kentucky, Maryland, and Missouri—stayed in the Union. In some towns in these border states, the Union and Confederate armies recruited volunteers on opposite sides of the same street. Kentucky, for example, provided 35,000 troops for the Southern armies, while 70,000 Kentuckians wore Union blue.

Opinion was divided within the free states as well. On the West Coast, some leading citizens in California and Oregon briefly considered seceding from the Union and forming a new nation. Civic leaders in Manhattan contemplated declaring New York a "free city," and there was talk of secession in New Jersey.

Some of the least-known fighting between supporters of the Union and the Confederacy took place in the vast, underpopulated territories of the West. Confederate forces seized much of the future states of Arizona and New Mexico in the early part of the war. Control of the region returned to the Union after clashes at Pichaco Pass, Arizona, in March 1862, and at La Glorietta Pass, New Mexico, in April. One Western territory, Nevada, was admitted to the Union in October 1864, largely because the North needed Nevada's mineral wealth to help finance its war effort.

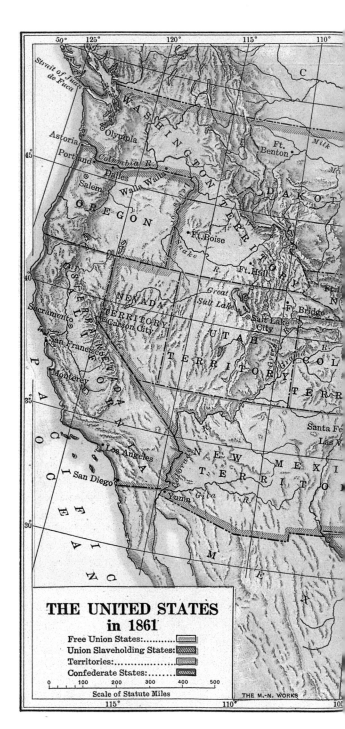

THE UNITED STATES in 1861

Free Union States:...........
Union Slaveholding States:
Territories:...............
Confederate States:........

0   100   200   300   400   500
Scale of Statute Miles

THE M.-N. WORKS

A TIMELINE OF MAJOR EVENTS
April 1861–August 1861

AT HOME AND ABROAD

April 15, 1861 President Lincoln calls for 75,000 state militia troops to crush the rebellion.

April 29 The legislature of the border state of Maryland, vital because of its proximity to Washington, D.C., votes to stay in the Union.

May 6 Arkansas joins the Confederacy.
•The Confederate government declares war on the U.S. (President Lincoln uses the term "insurrection," rather than war, to describe the conflict.)

May 15 Queen Victoria declares that Great Britain will remain neutral, although cotton from the South is considered vital to Britain's textile industry.

May 16 The Confederate government calls for the raising of a 400,000-man army to repel the expected invasion from the North.

May 20 Richmond, Virginia, becomes the capital of the Confederate States of America.

•North Carolina votes to join the Confederacy.
•Governor Magoffin of Kentucky announces that his state will remain neutral.

Confederate troops

MILITARY EVENTS

April 11, 1861 South Carolina authorities demand Fort Sumter's surrender. Its Union commander, Major Robert Anderson, refuses. Bombardment begins early on April 12; Anderson, out of food and water, finally surrenders the badly battered fort the next day.

April 18 Union general in chief Winfield Scott offers Colonel Robert E. Lee command of the Union Army being raised; Lee declines.
•The first regiment of volunteer Union troops (from Pennsylvania) arrives in Washington to assist the capital's defense.

April 19 A Massachusetts regiment traveling through Baltimore is attacked by a secessionist mob. Three soldiers and eleven civilians are killed in the riot that follows.

•President Lincoln declares a naval blockade of all Confederate ports.

May 3 General Winfield Scott outlines what is quickly called the "Anaconda Plan" to defeat the South; the strategy calls for the Union to first isolate and then strangle the Confederacy by a naval blockade combined with control of the Mississippi River.

May 10-11 Riots between pro-Union and secessionist mobs sweep St. Louis, Missouri. A determined effort by Captain Nathaniel Lyon defeats secessionist (pro-South) forces.

May 24 Union troops occupy Alexandria, Virginia; Colonel Elmer Ellsworth is killed while tearing down a Confederate flag. He becomes one of the first Union war heroes.

June 3 General George McClellan's

May 23 Virginia secedes from the Union.

May 27 Chief Justice Roger B. Taney declares Lincoln's suspension of habeas corpus (the right not to be held prisoner without charges or a trial) unconstitutional.

June 8 Tennessee votes to join the Confederacy, despite much pro-Union feeling in the state's eastern region. There are now eleven states in the Confederacy.

June 10 Napoleon III, the ruler of France, declares French neutrality—as in Britain, however, there is much pro-Confederate feeling in the government.
•The U.S. surgeon general appoints Dorothea Dix to supervise the Union Army's nurses. Dix is already well-known for her efforts to improve conditions in hospitals for the mentally ill.

June 19 Leading citizens of the western counties of Virginia meet at Wheeling and vote to stay in the Union, even if it involves forming a new state.

July 25 The U.S. Congress passes the Crittenden Resolution; it states that the Union's war aim is to crush the Southern rebellion, not to abolish slavery.

August 2 To meet the costs of the war, the U.S. Congress passes the first federal income tax in the nation's history.

August 30 John C. Frémont, military governor of Missouri, orders that the property of all pro-Confederate citizens be seized, including slaves. Lincoln later modifies the order in response to protests by anti-abolitionist Northern politicians.

troops defeat a Confederate force at Philippi, in western Virginia. This victory helps keep the largely pro-Union region from joining the Confederacy.

July 14 A large Union force under General Irwin McDowell leaves Washington and advances on the Confederate Army at Manassas Junction, Virginia.

July 21 The First Battle of Bull Run (called First Manassas in the South) is fought. After initial success, McDowell's army is defeated and the survivors begin a retreat to Washington.

August 10 Pro-Confederates defeat forces led by Nathaniel Lyon in the Battle of Wilson's Creek, Missouri. Lyon dies in the fighting.

August 20 General George McClellan assumes command of the Army of the Potomac, the largest Union fighting force.

August 27 Union land and naval forces capture Cape Hatteras on the North Carolina coast. The landing greatly strengthens the Union's blockade of Southern ports.

The charge on the plateau at Bull Run

A TIMELINE OF MAJOR EVENTS

September 1861–April 1862

AT HOME AND ABROAD

September 11 Realizing the impossibility of staying out of the war, Kentucky's state legislature orders all Confederate troops to leave the state.

September 17 In the first of many surprises in the Confederate cabinet, Attorney General Judah P. Benjamin is appointed secretary of war.

October 24 The first transcontinental telegraph message is sent from Sacramento, California, to Washington, D.C.

November 6 Jefferson Davis, president of the Confederacy by appointment, is formally elected to the post. Alexander Stephens becomes the Confederacy's vice president.

November 8 An American warship stops the British steamer *Trent* in the Atlantic and forcibly removes Confederate diplomats James Mason and John Slidell, who are en route to Europe to seek recognition for the Confederacy.

Judah P. Benjamin

November 30 The *Trent* affair becomes a full-blown international incident when the British government demands the release of Mason and Slidell.

December 20 Dissatisfied with President Lincoln's war effort, nine congressmen form the Joint Committee on the Conduct of the War.

December 26 After Britain sends troops to Canada, Secretary of State

MILITARY EVENTS

September 3 Confederate troops invade Kentucky. Union troops under General Ulysses S. Grant seize Paducah, Kentucky, three days later.

October 21 Union troops are defeated at Ball's Bluff on the Potomac River. Among those killed is Colonel Edward Baker, a senator from Oregon and a friend of President Lincoln.

November 1 General Winfield Scott

The capture of Roanoke Island

resigns as commander in chief of Union forces; General George McClellan assumes overall command of the Union war effort.

November 7 A combined army-navy operation leads to a Union capture of Port Royal, North Carolina.

January 19, 1862 Union troops drive Confederate forces from the eastern part of Kentucky in the Battle of Mill Springs.

February 6 General Grant's troops, assisted by gunboats commanded by Commodore Andrew Foote, capture Fort Henry on the Tennessee River.

February 8 A naval battle off Roanoke Island, North Carolina, ends in a Union victory; several Confederate forts and warships are destroyed, and Union troops, under General Ambrose Burnside, succeed in capturing the island.

William Seward orders the release of Mason and Slidell into British custody.

January 11, 1862 Lincoln appoints Senator Edwin Stanton to the post of secretary of war, replacing Simon Cameron.

January 31 Congress authorizes President Lincoln to seize railroad and telegraph lines for the war effort.

February 22 Jefferson Davis

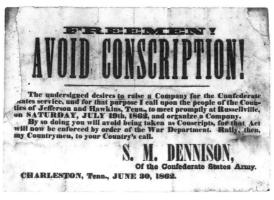

Broadside encouraging Confederate troops to enlist

and Alexander Stephens are inaugurated as president and vice president of the Confederate States of America.

March 4 President Lincoln appoints Andrew Johnson—a Southern Democrat loyal to the Union—to the post

of military governor of Tennessee.

March 6 Lincoln asks Congress to consider compensation for slave-owners in any state that voluntarily frees its slaves. The reaction from border state politicians is lukewarm.

April 16 The Confederate government authorizes conscription (drafting troops) to fill the ranks of its armies.

February 12 General Grant begins a siege of Fort Donelson, located on the Tennessee River.

February 16 Confederate general Simon Bolívar Buckner surrenders Fort Donelson to Grant. The victory makes Grant a hero in the North.

March 7–8 The Battle of Pea Ridge, the most important clash west of the Mississippi River, is fought in Arkansas. Union forces under General

Samuel Curtis suffer heavy casualties, but Confederate general Earl Van Dorn's troops withdraw to the Mississippi River.

March 8 Two Union warships are sunk and several others are damaged off Hampton Roads, Virginia, by the Confederate ironclad *Merrimack*.

March 9 The Union ironclad *Monitor* engages the *Merrimack* in combat off Hampton Roads. Their three-hour

fight, the first battle ever fought by ironclads, ends when the *Merrimack* moves out of the *Monitor*'s range.

March 17 The Peninsular Campaign begins as the first transports carrying Union forces leave Alexandria. McClellan plans to land on the peninsula between Virginia's York and James rivers and move inland to capture Richmond.

April 6–7 The Battle of Shiloh (called

the Battle of Pittsburg Landing in the South) is fought in Tennessee. Grant's troops hold out after a bloody two-day attack.

April 25 A Union naval expedition, led by Commodore David Farragut, captures New Orleans. The loss of the South's largest city and outlet to the Gulf of Mexico is a major blow for the Confederacy.

A TIMELINE OF MAJOR EVENTS

May 1862–December 1862

AT HOME AND ABROAD

May 16 General Benjamin Butler, commander of the Union forces occupying New Orleans, issues an order stating that women who show disrespect to Union troops will be treated as prostitutes. The order sparks outrage in the South.

May 17 A major uprising of Santee Sioux Indians, led by Chief Little Crow, begins in western Minnesota; thousands of white settlers flee their homes until federal and state troops arrive to rout the Indians.

June 19 Congress outlaws slavery in all the territories in the West.

July 1–2 Congress passes two far-reaching laws: The first formally authorizes the building of a transcontinental railroad; the second, the Morrill Act, gives federal land to states in order to pay for the building of colleges.

Little Crow

July 22 President Lincoln writes the first draft of the document which will become the Emancipation Proclamation. He tells his cabinet he will wait until the Union scores a major victory before announcing the measure.

August 22 In a public letter to newspaper editor Horace Greeley, President Lincoln states that his chief war aim is to reunite the nation, not destroy slavery—in spite of

MILITARY EVENTS

May 8 Fast-moving Confederate troops under General Thomas "Stonewall" Jackson beat Union forces at McDowell, Virginia, in one of the opening battles of Jackson's legendary Shenandoah Valley Campaign.

June 6 Memphis, Tennessee, surrenders to Union forces after seven Confederate ironclads are destroyed in a naval battle on the Mississippi River.

June 8–9 After victories at Cross Keys and Port Republic, Virginia, Stonewall Jackson leaves the Shenandoah Valley to help General Lee defend Richmond from McClellan's advancing army.

June 25 The major phase of the Peninsular Campaign, the Seven Days Battles, begins. •McClellan's advance on Richmond is stalled in the face of stiff Confederate resistance, but the Army of the Potomac conducts a fighting retreat through eastern Virginia.

July 1 The Seven Days Battles end when Union forces reach the safety of Malvern Hill, where they beat back a Confederate assault with artillery.

August 29–30 The Second Battle of Bull Run is fought at Manassas, Virginia. The Army of the Potomac is defeated by Lee and Jackson.

September 5 Confederate forces begin crossing the Potomac River into Maryland, beginning the Confederacy's first invasion of the North. Lincoln reinstates McClellan as commander of the Army of the Potomac to deal with the threat.

September 17 The Battle of Antietam is fought near

the upcoming Emancipation Proclamation.

September 22 Following the Confederate retreat from Antietam, President Lincoln delivers the Emancipation Proclamation. It states that as of January 1, 1863, all slaves living in Confederate-held territory will be considered "forever free."

November Many Republican candidates are defeated in Congressional elections in the North. This outcome is considered a sign that the Northern public is losing confidence in the Lincoln administration.

December 1 In a message to Congress, President Lincoln again proposes a plan to compensate landowners for releasing their slaves.

December 18–20 Secretary of State William Seward and Secretary of the Treasury Sal-

Salmon Chase

mon Chase offer their resignations; both cabinet members were accused of playing a role in the Union defeat at Fredericksburg. Lincoln refuses their resignations.

December 28 Thirty-eight Sioux Indians are executed at Mankato, Minnesota, for their role in the Santee Uprising. Over 300 Indians were originally sentenced to death, but Lincoln overturns most of the convictions.

December 31 Congress agrees to admit those Virginia counties that are pro-Union as a new state, to be called West Virginia.

Sharpsburg, Maryland. The bloodiest day of the Civil War ends with Lee's invasion halted; more than 25,000 Union and Confederate soldiers are killed, wounded, or captured in the fighting.

The Battle of Fredericksburg

October 4–6 The Confederate advance in the war's Western Theater slows as forces under Union general William Rosecrans defeat a Confederate force near Corinth, Mississippi.

November 4 General Grant begins a campaign to capture Vicksburg, Mississippi.

November 5 General Ambrose Burnside becomes commander of the Army of the Potomac.

December 11 Union forces cross the Rappahannock River in the opening move of a campaign intended to capture Fredericksburg, Virginia.

December 13 In the Battle of Fredericksburg, Burnside's attempt to storm the high ground around the city ends in a defeat for the Union.

December 31 The Battle of Murfreesboro begins in Tennessee as Confederate forces under General Braxton Bragg attack positions held by Union troops led by General William Rosecrans.

Part I
The Blue and the Gray

This patriotic lithograph applauds the Northerners who answered Lincoln's call for volunteers following the attack on Fort Sumter. Believing that the war would be quickly won, the Union allowed volunteers to sign up for ninety-day enlistments. As a result, several volunteer regiments went home the evening before the First Battle of Bull Run in July 1861.

The day after the South's attack on Fort Sumter, Union president Abraham Lincoln called for volunteers to fight the Confederacy. The Civil War had begun. The North's goal at this early stage was not to free the slaves, but to restore the Union, although many Northern politicians soon called for the freeing of slaves in captured territory. Lincoln firmly refused to acknowledge the Confederacy as an independent nation. Although he declared a blockade of Southern ports and ordered that captured Confederates be treated as prisoners of war, Lincoln saw the conflict as a rebellion, not a war between two countries.

The Civil War quickly became three wars. The first was fought east of the Appalachian Mountains, mainly in Virginia. Here, the Union objective was to capture Richmond, the capital of the Confederacy. (According to nineteenth-century military strategy, the capture of cities, rather than the destruction of armies, was the key to victory.) But the North's hope for a quick victory vanished in July 1861, when the Confederates defeated a Union advance on Richmond at Bull Run, the first major battle of the war.

The second war took place in the region between the Appalachian Mountains and the Mississippi River. Here the Union was more successful. By 1862, Union victories in the West began to split the Confederacy in two. But success sometimes proved costly; the heavy casualties at the Battle of Shiloh, fought on April 6–7, 1862, shocked the North. In the same month, however, New Orleans, the South's gateway to the Gulf of Mexico, fell to the Union Navy.

The third war was the war at sea. In this conflict, the North won important victories in 1861 and 1862, as the Union Navy seized bases on the Southern coast to tighten its blockade and cut the Confederacy off from overseas help.

THE SHOOTING BEGINS: FORT SUMTER

P.G.T. Beauregard of Louisiana, the first brigadier general of the Confederate Army, received the order to fire on Fort Sumter shortly before dawn on April 12, 1861. For thirty-three hours the batteries around Charleston Harbor poured more than 4,000 shells at the fort. The city's residents watched excitedly from their rooftops.

Finally, at 2:30 on the afternoon of April 13, the fort's commander, Major Robert Anderson, surrendered. The seventy-three-man garrison marched out and lowered the American flag. Anderson ordered the fort's guns fired in a final salute. A spark landed in a sack of gunpowder; it exploded, killing Private Daniel Hough, the only casualty of the siege and the first death of the war. Confederate authorities allowed Anderson and his troops to board a Union ship waiting outside the harbor. As the ship steamed north, the Confederates on shore saluted in tribute to the bravery of the defenders.

With the attack on Fort Sumter, the long-brewing Civil War began in earnest. As news of the fort's surrender clicked along the telegraph lines of the North, most people expressed determination to put down the Southern rebellion.

Reactions in the South were mixed. Many greeted the victory with cheers and celebrations. Others, especially in the states that hadn't yet joined the Confederacy, were grim. "We must," said one Virginian, "[now] identify ourselves with the North or the South."

This Charleston newspaper (above) announces the surrender of "Fort Sumpter." It also notes that Major Anderson is a prisoner of war. In actuality, Confederate authorities decided to allow the fort's garrison to travel north after they surrendered.

This lithograph (right) shows Confederate shore batteries pounding Fort Sumter on the early morning of April 12, 1861. Despite thirty-three hours of shelling, the Union garrison surrendered only after fires threatened to spread to the fort's store of gunpowder.

Major Robert Anderson (1805–71) was a Southerner—a native of Kentucky. His family came from Virginia and his wife was from Georgia. His gallant defense of Fort Sumter, however, made him a hero in the North. After the fort's surrender, he went to Kentucky to rally support for the Union cause among its divided population.

THE NORTH PREPARES FOR WAR

On April 14, 1861, President Abraham Lincoln called for 75,000 volunteer troops to enlist for ninety days in order to put down the rebellion. State governments were to provide these troops by enlisting them in their militias. At the time the war broke out, however, most state militia units were little more than social organizations.

In the wave of anger that followed Fort Sumter, thousands of patriotic young men swamped Northern recruiting offices. Most states filled their quotas right away, except for the border states of the upper South and the West. The governor of Kentucky said that his state would "furnish no troops for the wicked purpose of subduing her sister Southern states." Missouri's governor told Lincoln, "Your requisition is illegal, unconstitutional, revolutionary, inhuman . . ."

The North had to rely on volunteer forces because the existing army numbered only about 16,000 men, most of whom were scattered in small forts in the far West. Also, a high percentage of Union Army officers were Southern-born. Eventually, more than a third of them "went South" when their native states left the Union. Not one of the army's enlisted men, however, deserted to join the Confederates.

The volunteers were organized into regiments of about a thousand men each. Discipline was lax in most of these early volunteer regiments. In some, the enlisted men even elected their own officers.

Taken from an 1861 map, this small gallery of "Military Portraits" (right) depicts some of the Union's highest-ranking generals in the first year of the war. The variety in uniforms worn by volunteer troops in the war's early stages can be seen in the illustrations along the print's borders.

Many early volunteers arrived in Washington wearing fancy uniforms. Some, called "Zouaves," copied the colorful, baggy-trousered clothes used by French Colonial troops in North Africa, as depicted in these labels (below) from packets of tobacco. Most Zouave units eventually adopted the regular Union Army dress—a dark blue tunic and sky-blue trousers.

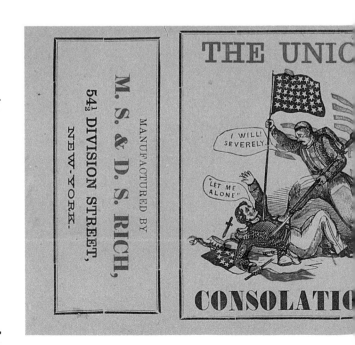

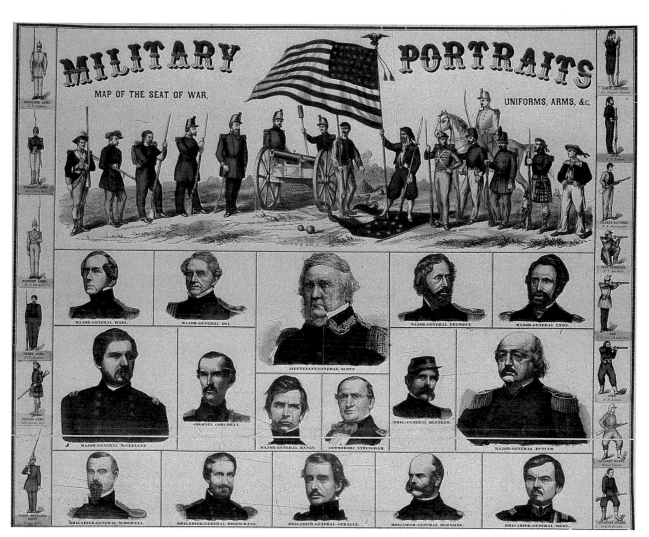

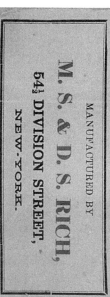

THE SOUTH PREPARES FOR WAR

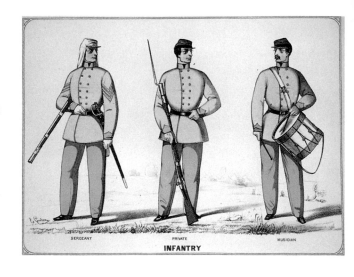

INFANTRY

In 1861, the North and the South appeared to be unequal opponents. The population of the Union was more than twice that of the Confederacy. There were 110,000 factories in the North; 18,000 in the South. The North possessed most of America's wealth, and its diverse economy could adapt to war—unlike the South, which relied almost completely on crop exports.

Still, many Southerners were confident that the Confederacy could fight, and win, a war with the North. The South had a smaller population, but slaves made up much of its labor force, freeing white men to join the army. In contrast to the "greasy mechanics" of the North, many Southern men were used to riding, shooting, and living an outdoor life. Southerners cheerfully predicted that "one rebel was the equal of ten Yankees." Most important, the Confederacy needed only to defend its territory to win its independence. The North would have to invade and wage war in a hostile country to put down the rebellion.

As the Southern states seceded, their governments seized federal military property, including forts and stocks of weapons. In some cases they didn't have to use force.

Confederate president Jefferson Davis, a soldier by training, moved quickly to put the Confederacy on solid footing for war. In early 1861, he called for an army of 100,000 men; by the time of the attack on Fort Sumter, the South had 60,000 men under arms.

The Confederacy's standard uniform was similar to the Union's, but was gray instead of blue. The sergeant at left in this print (above) wears headgear known as a "havelock." Designed to protect the wearer's face and neck from the sun, it was copied from the British Army in India. Most Confederate soldiers, however, preferred a soft-brimmed "slouch" hat.

Because of supply and manufacturing problems, Confederate troops wore a wide variety of uniforms. Many didn't even wear gray; the most common fabric was a brownish homespun called "butternut." This 1861 photograph (opposite, top) of Confederate volunteers at Pensacola, Florida, shows soldiers in many different uniforms.

The Confederate Army's weapons and equipment were inferior to the Union's in many ways, but the South never lacked skillful fighting commanders. This lithograph (right) depicts the Confederacy's highest-ranking generals grouped around President Jefferson Davis (center), himself a West Point graduate and a distinguished veteran of the Mexican War.

WASHINGTON

In early 1861, a Virginia newspaper called Washington, D.C., a "filthy cage of unclean birds" that "must and will be purified." In the days after Fort Sumter, it did seem that the Union capital would soon be "purified" by Confederate troops. Washington was surrounded on one of its four sides by Virginia and on the other three by Maryland. These states were still in the Union, but in both, secessionist feeling was running high. From the White House, President Lincoln could see Confederate flags fluttering on the heights at Arlington, Virginia. "Why don't they come?" he asked his wife, Mary, referring to the 75,000 volunteers he had called for on April 14.

The only major rail connection to Washington ran through the mostly pro-Confederate city of Baltimore. On April 19, the 6th Massachusetts Regiment, one of the first militia units to answer Lincoln's call, was attacked by a pro-Confederate mob while passing through the city. The 6th Regiment fired on the crowd. Four soldiers died, along with several civilians. After the riot, Maryland secessionists cut the telegraph lines, ripped up rails, and burned bridges over the Potomac River. Washington was now almost completely isolated.

A few days later, however, Massachusetts militia general Benjamin Butler opened a path to Washington by way of Annapolis, Maryland. By the end of April, 10,000 troops had arrived in the city, allowing Lincoln to reestablish control of Baltimore and both sides of the Potomac River.

The dome over the Capitol building (above) was only half finished when President Abraham Lincoln took office in 1861. Lincoln ordered construction to continue, despite the cost; the dome symbolized his hope that the divided Union would one day be reunited. The 1,000-ton structure was finally completed in 1863.

Keeping military secrets was difficult in Washington. To improve security, General George McClellan issued an order in September 1861, "prohibiting civilians and others not on duty from crossing the [Potomac] river without permits from headquarters." This photograph (opposite, top) shows Union sentries checking passes at the ferry linking Georgetown, in the District of Columbia, with Virginia.

Washington was linked to the sea by the Potomac River—as shown in this view (right) by a Baltimore lithographer. Because the Union capital was so close to the Confederacy, thousands of troops had to be kept along the Potomac to protect the city from invasion. In addition, many forts were soon built around the city.

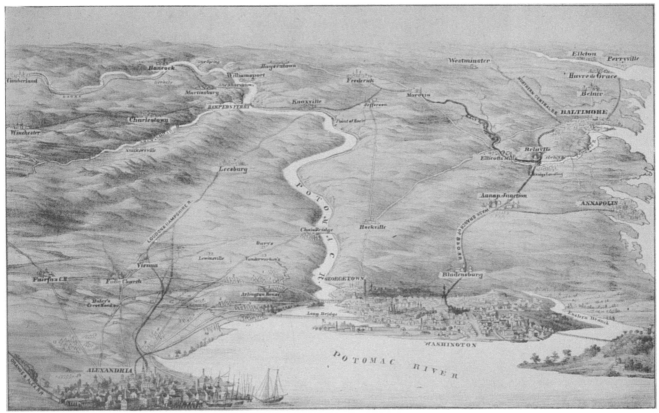

THE BORDER STATES

At the time of the attack on Fort Sumter, the Confederacy included seven states—Alabama, Florida, Georgia, Louisiana, Mississippi, South Carolina, and Texas. The border states—slave-holding states between the North and the states of the lower South—had at first declined to leave the Union, until war finally came.

An Arkansas state convention voted for secession on May 6, 1861. North Carolina was the next state to leave: Its state legislature passed an ordinance of secession on May 20. Tennessee followed early in June.

Kentucky announced that it would remain "neutral" in the conflict. Missouri's government favored secession, but did not formally withdraw. Both states did have provisional Confederate governments, and they were represented by the Confederate flag.

Delaware, although officially a slave state, had only a handful of slaves among its small population and voted to stay in the Union. Maryland had many pro-Confederate citizens, especially in Baltimore, where more than one third of the state's population lived. But the presence of the Northern military and the actions of loyal citizens kept Maryland in the Union.

Virginia, traditionally the South's leader, chose to secede. It was the most populous state and home to most of the region's industry. On April 17, the state convention passed an ordinance of secession, subject to a statewide vote. When the vote took place on May 23, Virginians voted overwhelmingly for secession.

One of the most vocal supporters of Virginia's secession was Edmund Ruffin (opposite), who (according to
tradition) fired the first shot at Fort Sumter. An agricul-
tural scientist, Ruffin admired the efficient farms of the
free states but hated everything else about the North.
He committed suicide in June 1865, following the defeat of his beloved South.

Some of the most bitter fighting of the Civil War took
place in Western border states such as Arkansas and
Missouri, the area shown in this map (below). Missouri, in a historian's words, became a "no-man's land
of hit-and-run raids, ambush, arson, and murder."
Some of the Old West's most notorious outlaws, including Jesse and Frank James and Cole Younger, were
Confederate "bushwhackers" in Missouri during the
war.

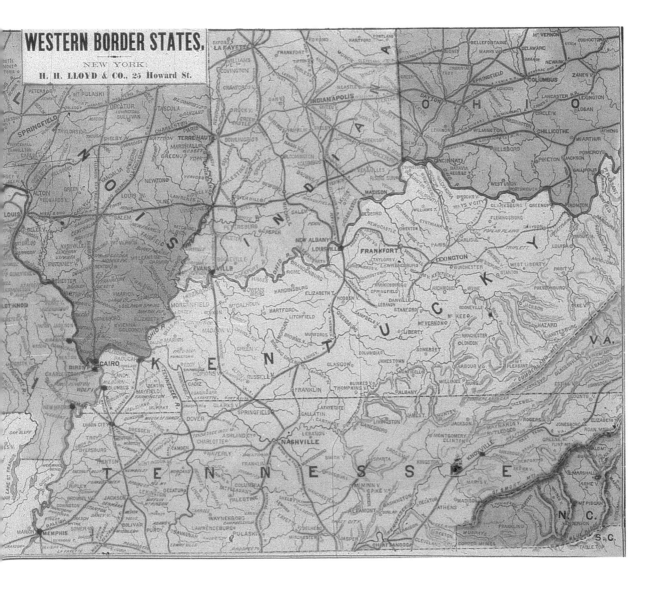

RICHMOND

Even before the state voted to secede, Virginia's leaders had invited the Confederate government to move from Montgomery, Alabama, to Richmond, the capital of Virginia.

In 1861, Richmond's population was about 38,000. Its importance was economic and political. It contained the huge Tredegar Iron Works, one of the few factories in the South capable of producing modern weapons. Most of the upper South's major wagon and railroad routes passed through the city. Richmond was close to the arsenal at Harpers Ferry and the Gosport Navy Yard, two important federal posts seized by Virginia secessionists after the attack on Fort Sumter.

But Richmond was only about 100 miles from Washington, D.C. President Davis, deciding that the city was not a safe place for the Confederate government, at first turned down Virginia's offer. Confederate politicians, however, persuaded him to accept. They believed that Montgomery was too small and remote a city to serve as the new nation's capital.

Davis arrived in Richmond on May 29. In a speech to the cheering crowd that greeted him, he said, "The country relies upon you . . . I have only to say, my friends, that to the last breath of my life I am wholly yours."

Moving the Confederate government to Richmond was significant to Civil War strategy. For nearly four years, a series of Union commanders tried again and again to capture the enemy capital that was so close to their own, while Confederate generals fought desperately to protect it.

Refusing the offer of a special train, Jefferson Davis (above) traveled from Montgomery to Richmond aboard an ordinary passenger coach. Festive, confident crowds greeted the president at every stop between the two cities. One observer called Davis's journey a "continuous ovation."

The "White House of the Confederacy"—it was actually gray in color—was Jefferson Davis's mansion on Clay Street in Richmond. Davis, his wife Varina, and their three children (joined by a fourth in 1862) moved to the house shortly after Richmond became the Confederate capital.

This aerial view of Richmond shows the position of the Confederate capital between the James and Chickahominy rivers. The artist has included scenes from the Union campaign to seize Richmond in the spring and summer of 1862, when the Northern forces were split by the rain-swollen Chickahominy.

EARLY STRATEGY

In April 1861, the commander of the U.S. Army was General in Chief Winfield Scott (1786–1866), a seventy-four-year-old hero of the War of 1812 and the Mexican War. In the first months of the war, he outlined the strategy that would eventually lead to a Union victory. Unfortunately, Northern military and political leaders ignored much of his advice.

On May 3, Scott presented his plan to President Lincoln. Instead of directly attacking the Confederacy, Scott wanted to surround it. He called for the Navy to blockade Southern ports on the coasts of the Atlantic and the Gulf of Mexico. This would prevent Southern cotton from getting out and foreign aid from getting in. At the same time, gunboats and soldiers would take control of the Mississippi River, cutting off the Confederacy from the West. Squeezed on both sides, the Confederacy would have to surrender or starve. Scott estimated that it would take hundreds of thousands of troops and several years to strangle the Confederacy into surrender.

Many Northerners, especially in the press, ridiculed Scott's strategy. They dubbed it the "Anaconda Plan," after the giant snake that strangles its prey. Some hinted that Scott (a Virginian by birth) was a Southern sympathizer intentionally misleading the Union. They pointed out that the Confederate capital at Richmond was less than a hundred miles from Washington. Capture Richmond, said Scott's critics, and the Confederacy would collapse. The *New York Tribune* summed up this view with a bold headline: "Forward to Richmond!"

An Ohio journalist sketched this cartoon of "Scott's Great Snake." Despite its crudeness, the drawing accurately represents Winfield Scott's plan to strangle the Confederacy economically as well as on the battlefield. It places the snake's upper half far to the west of the Mississippi River, a key goal of Union strategy.

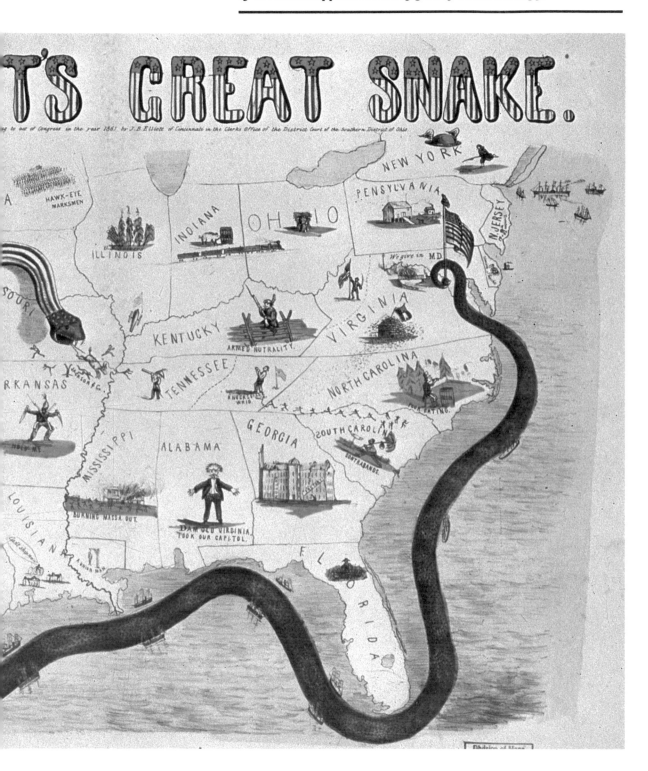

EARLY CLASHES: THE EAST

Few major battles took place east of the Appalachian Mountains in the spring of 1861. The Union command's first concern—besides raising, supplying, and training an effective army—was to make Washington secure.

On May 24, Union troops occupied Arlington, Virginia, just across the Potomac River from Washington. When Colonel Elmer Ellsworth pulled down a Confederate flag flying over the town's hotel, the hotel keeper, James Jackson, shot and killed him. Union troops then killed Jackson.

The first true battle of the war in the East took place at Big Bethel, Virginia, along the James River. On June 10, troops under General Benjamin Butler attacked a smaller Confederate force under Confederate colonel John B. Magruder. Butler's inexperienced troops panicked under fire and the attack failed.

The main Union military effort was in western, not eastern, Virginia. When Virginia seceded, its mountainous western counties, with few slaves and a strongly pro-Union population, refused to go along. Confederate troops under General Robert Garnett moved in to keep the region in Confederate hands. In the summer of 1861, Union forces, led by generals George B. McClellan and William S. Rosecrans, moved down from Ohio to throw the Confederates out. A campaign of small battles, fought mostly for control of mountain passes, followed. After Union victories at Philippi, Rich Mountain, and Carrick's Ford, the Confederates withdrew.

General John B. Magruder (1810–71; above), Confederate commander at Big Bethel, was an amateur actor in the pre-war U.S. Army. During the Peninsular Campaign of 1862, Magruder put his stage skills to military use. By marching his men back and forth over the same spot, Magruder convinced Union commanders that his troops far outnumbered their forces.

The print shown here (opposite, top) depicts a Union column advancing through one of western Virginia's rugged mountain passes in the spring of 1861. A Northern soldier described the region as "a land of secession, rattlesnakes, rough mountains, and bad whiskey." The North gained control of the region by the summer, but guerrilla fighting continued until the war's end.

The engraving shown here (right) originally appeared in Harper's Weekly, one of the North's leading journals. It depicts Union Zouaves charging into combat at Big Bethel, Virginia. Although this was a mere skirmish compared with battles to come, the Confederate victory, in the words of a Southern writer, "showed to the boasting North how terribly we were in earnest."

EARLY CLASHES: THE WEST

West of the Appalachian Mountains, the struggle to keep Kentucky and Missouri in the Union continued. At first, Kentucky's government called for a policy of "strict neutrality." But neither side could accept such a position. Kentucky's governor, Beriah Magoffin, was pro-Confederate, but the state legislature was mostly pro-Union. The state's population was also divided between the two sides.

In early September 1861, Confederate troops moved into Kentucky from Tennessee and occupied Columbus. Shortly afterward, Union troops occupied Paducah and Smithland. Faced with this dual invasion, Kentucky's legislature passed a resolution ordering the Confederate forces out of the state. Secessionist Kentuckians then organized a state convention which voted to join the Confederacy. At the end of 1861, the southwest corner of Kentucky remained in Confederate hands, while the Union controlled the rest of the state.

Like Kentucky, Missouri belonged to the Union at the start of the war, yet its government and people were deeply divided. The state militia supported pro-Confederate governor Claiborne Jackson. To keep the state in the Union, U.S. Army captain Nathaniel Lyon scraped together a pro-Union force that gained control of St. Louis. On August 10, however, Confederate militia defeated pro-Union forces in the Battle of Wilson's Creek. Lyon was killed in the battle, but the Union managed to keep hold of Missouri.

Although only a captain, Nathaniel Lyon (1818–61; right) found himself the senior Union officer in Missouri when Confederates captured General William S. Harney. Before the fighting in St. Louis, Lyon made a personal reconnaissance through the Confederate stronghold at Camp Jackson disguised as a woman—despite his bushy red beard.

The Union cause in Missouri suffered a major setback in August 1861, when 6,000 men led by Nathaniel Lyon clashed with 12,000 Confederates under General Sterling Price at Wilson's Creek. Although wounded, Lyon stayed on the battlefield to rally his troops. When a second Southern bullet killed him, as shown in this engraving, the Union line collapsed and retreated.

THE FIRST MAJOR BATTLE: BULL RUN

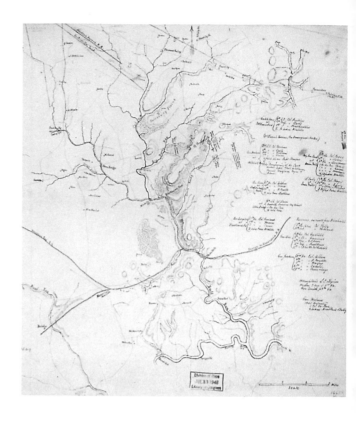

By the summer of 1861, President Lincoln came under increasing pressure to move against the Confederacy. Newspapers and politicians clamored for the capture of Richmond, believing that one big battle would crush the Confederacy and restore the Union.

By July, there were about 35,000 Union troops in and around Washington. Lincoln ordered their commander, General Irvin S. McDowell, to attack the 20,000 Confederate soldiers at Manassas Junction in Virginia and to begin an advance on Richmond.

On July 13, McDowell's army left Alexandria, Virginia, on the march to Manassas. The undisciplined, inexperienced soldiers moved slowly, and the roads were clogged with carriages full of civilians traveling from Washington to watch the battle. It took the Union troops five days to reach Centreville, about three miles from Manassas.

Confederate general P.G.T. Beauregard knew McDowell was coming. The slow Union march gave him time to rush thousands of reinforcements to Manassas and to build up a defensive line along a stream called Bull Run.

The Union assault began on the morning of July 21. McDowell hit the Confederates miles from where they had expected the attack to come, and the Southerners fell back. By afternoon, Union forces had crossed Bull Run and advanced south of Warrenton Turnpike, the road connecting Washington and Richmond. Victory seemed within McDowell's grasp.

This map (above) shows the area around Manassas Junction, the site of the first major confrontation between Union and Confederate forces. Northern commander Irvin McDowell (1818–85) personally scouted the terrain around Bull Run a day before the battle.

Some 150,000 Americans of Irish birth or parentage fought for the Union. One of the first Irish units to see action was the 69th New York, better known as the "Fighting Irish." This lithograph (opposite, top) shows the 69th, led by Colonel Michael Corcoran, charging Confederate cannons at Bull Run.

Oxen pull artillery into position at Manassas in this drawing (right) by a Confederate officer. Manassas Junction's strategic location at the meeting point of several important roads and railroads allowed General P.G.T. Beauregard to move men and weapons into position to face McDowell's advancing army.

A Confederate Bull Battery previous to the Battle of Bull Run

FIRST BULL RUN: THE OUTCOME

McDowell's battle plan was probably too complicated for his half-trained officers and men. The Confederates rallied and fought back hard. As soon as it ran into serious resistance, the Union advance crumbled into a series of unconnected attacks and counterattacks. The gun smoke, the similar uniforms worn by some units on both sides, and the shock of battle on inexperienced troops led to total confusion.

As the hot July sun began to sink, the Union troops started to fall back. As more Confederate reinforcements reached the battlefield, thousands of Union soldiers fled, some throwing down their rifles in panic. "The farther they ran, the more frightened they grew," said a Union congressman who watched the battle. By evening, retreating troops jammed the roads back to Washington. Fleeing with them were the frightened civilians who had come to Manassas with picnic lunches and champagne to see the Union Army "whip the rebels."

By the standards of later battles, the Battle of Bull Run (the South called it the Battle of Manassas) was little more than a skirmish. The Confederate Army lost about 2,000 men, both killed and wounded. Union casualties were roughly equal, with 1,200 captured. But the battle's effect on Northern public opinion was great. Hopes for a short war disappeared overnight. Horace Greeley, the New York newspaper editor who had called for an advance on Richmond, even proposed that Lincoln "make peace with the rebels, and on their own terms."

General Thomas J. Jackson (1824–63; above) won his famous nickname, "Stonewall," at Bull Run. When his brigade of Virginians held fast against a Union charge on Henry House Hill, Confederate general Barnard Bee called out to his men, "There is Jackson standing like a stone wall!" (Some historians believe Bee added the word "damned" before "stone wall," and that he was actually angry at Jackson for not coming to his aid.)

P.G.T. Beauregard (1818–93) became the most popular of the South's early generals because of his victorious leadership at Fort Sumter and Bull Run. Shown here (opposite, top) is the sheet-music cover to a song, "Beauregard's March," composed in honor of the Louisiana-born general.

To increase discipline, Union officers put their units—such as the 96th Pennsylvania, shown here (right) at Camp Northumberland outside Washington—through hours of marching and drill. "There are a good many troops hanging on about the camps and forts on the other side of the [Potomac] river," wrote an English journalist after Bull Run, "but they are thoroughly disorganized."

THE ARMY OF THE POTOMAC

On the Monday after Bull Run, President Lincoln telegraphed Major General George Brinton McClellan to come to Washington and take command of the disheartened Union Army.

Only thirty-five years old, McClellan was a West Point graduate and a veteran of the Mexican War. After Fort Sumter, McClellan won several small battles in western Virginia. Lincoln hoped the handsome, energetic young general would turn the Union Army into an effective fighting force.

Throughout the summer of 1861, McClellan took thousands of inexperienced Union volunteers, drilling, training, and marching them until their morale and fighting skill soared. The troops of the Union Army in the East—now called the Army of the Potomac—loved "Little Mac."

But some parts of McClellan's personality troubled Lincoln and other Union leaders. McClellan was arrogant. He cared little for the president, even calling him "the original gorilla" in letters to his wife. Republicans in Congress distrusted McClellan, who was a Democrat.

McClellan also seemed reluctant to take his army into battle. Throughout the fall of 1861, Lincoln urged McClellan to move into Virginia. The general, convinced that the Confederates outnumbered his army, continually made excuses. Even so, when General in Chief Winfield Scott retired in November, Lincoln gave McClellan overall command of the Union forces, plus command of the Army of the Potomac.

A heroic General George McClellan (1826–85; right) points his sword toward the enemy in this 1861 lithograph. Some newspapers called him the "young Napoleon" because of his resemblance in height to the French emperor.

By the spring and summer of 1862, the Army of the Potomac numbered more than 100,000 men; McClellan needed 4,300 wagons and ambulances to carry the army's supplies and wounded. This lithograph (below) shows some of those wagons crossing Bear Run during the Union's retreat after the Peninsula Campaign.

THE *TRENT* AFFAIR

The Confederate government hoped that Britain and France would recognize the Confederacy as an independent nation and aid its war effort. After the attack on Fort Sumter, however, both European governments announced that they would remain neutral. In October 1861, President Davis sent two Confederate diplomats—James Mason of Virginia and John Slidell of Louisiana—to Europe in an effort to persuade Britain and France to reconsider.

Mason and Slidell first traveled to Cuba, where they boarded a British steamer, the *Trent*. Soon after it sailed, the Union warship *San Jacinto* appeared. Its commander, Captain Charles Wilkes, fired across the *Trent's* bow to stop it. A boarding party then removed Mason and Slidell at gunpoint. A few days later the two Confederate commissioners were sent to a Massachusetts prison.

The British government was outraged. One of its ships had been attacked in international waters—a clear violation of neutrality. The prime minister, Lord Palmerston, sent the Union government a letter demanding an apology and the release of Mason and Slidell. He also sent 10,000 British troops to Canada.

President Lincoln now faced the possibility of having to fight the British Empire in addition to the Confederacy. Reluctantly, he ordered Secretary of State William Seward to write an apology to Palmerston. On January 1, 1862, the Union released Mason and Slidell into British custody.

James Mason (1798–1871; above, top) came from a distinguished Virginia family, but his manners were hardly aristocratic. In her diary, Mary Chesnut—wife of South Carolina senator James Chesnut—wrote, "My wildest imagination will not picture him as a diplomat. He will say 'chaw' for chew, and call himself 'Jeems' . . . "

Born in New York, John Slidell (1793–1871; above, bottom) moved to the South and made his fortune as a sugar trader in New Orleans, where he became the brother-in-law of P.G.T. Beauregard. Because Slidell spoke French, Jefferson Davis gave him the job of persuading the emperor of France, Napoleon III, to support the Confederacy.

This engraving depicts Captain Charles Wilkes (1798–1877) ordering Mason and Slidell off the Trent. *Wilkes, a veteran of four decades in the U.S. Navy, made the capture of the two Confederate diplomats a personal quest. Although Wilkes acted without authorization, Congress passed a resolution thanking him for his action.*

FORT HENRY AND FORT DONELSON

In 1862, the Union turned its attention to the land west of the Appalachian Mountains, where about 50,000 Confederate troops held a 600-mile line ending at the Mississippi River. The key links in this defensive chain were two Tennessee forts: Fort Henry on the Tennessee River and Fort Donelson on the Cumberland River.

The Union commanders in the West, General Henry W. Halleck and General Don Carlos Buell, wanted both forts captured as the first step in a campaign to win control of the Mississippi. Forty-year-old Ulysses S. Grant, a brigadier general, asked for the job. In February, Grant and 15,000 troops set out from Cairo, Illinois, aboard a fleet of transports and gunboats commanded by Commodore Andrew H. Foote.

The Union forces reached Fort Henry on February 6. After shelling by Foote's gunboats, Confederate general Lloyd Tilghman ordered most of his 3,400 men to withdraw to Fort Donelson. Tilghman led a delaying action to cover his troops' escape, then surrendered Fort Henry to Grant.

Fort Donelson was defended by 12,000 Confederates. But after a brief siege, the fort's commander, General John B. Floyd, asked for surrender terms. Grant announced he would accept no terms but "unconditional and immediate surrender." On February 16, Floyd gave in.

The capture of forts Henry and Donelson drove a wedge into the heart of the Confederacy. It also brought U. S. Grant to the attention of the Union high command.

General Henry W. Halleck (1815–72; above), commander of the Union's Department of the West in 1862, was known as "Old Brains" for his writings on military topics. Lincoln made him general in chief in July 1862, but his ability as a commander never matched his reputation as a scholar. One Union officer called him "a vast emptiness surrounded by an education."

Together, Commodore Foote's gunboats mounted forty-eight heavy guns, and at 11:00 on the morning of February 6, they began pounding Fort Henry, as shown in this engraving (opposite, top) from a Northern newspaper. A great believer in army-navy cooperation, Andrew H. Foote (1806–63) said that troops and warships are "like the blades of shears—united, invincible; separated, useless."

General Grant (1822–85), shown on horseback in this painting (right), watches as his men go into action at Fort Donelson. The Northern press made much of the news that Grant demanded the fort's "unconditional surrender," because his initials were "U. S." In fact, Grant's original name was Hiram Ulysses. A clerical error at West Point listed him as "Ulysses Simpson," and Grant never corrected the mistake.

THE BATTLE OF SHILOH

After the Union victories at forts Henry and Donelson, Grant led his troops south down the Tennessee River. His goal was the road-and-railroad junction at Corinth, Mississippi. By the end of March 1862, Grant's army was camped at Pittsburg Landing, just north of the Mississippi border.

The Confederate commanders in the West—generals Albert Sidney Johnston, P.G.T. Beauregard, and Braxton Bragg—were willing to risk anything to stop Grant's advance. Moving north from Corinth with 40,000 troops, the Confederates launched their attack on the morning of April 6 near a Methodist church called Shiloh.

Grant's army was unprepared for the assault, having set up camp with no thought of defense or security. First companies, then whole regiments, of Union soldiers fled in panic as the Confederates swept forward. General William Tecumseh Sherman's troops temporarily held up the Confederate advance before retreating.

Grant hurried to the battlefield as soon as he heard gunfire. In pain from a leg injured in a riding accident, he personally rallied his troops. The battle quickly turned into what one historian called "a hundred furious little conflicts," as pockets of Union troops fought fiercely to hold their ground. The hail of bullets was so thick in one corner of the battlefield that it came to be called "The Hornet's Nest." Thousands of other Union soldiers, however, fled the battlefield to shelter under the bluffs at the edge of the Tennessee River.

In this scene (above) from the Battle of Shiloh, Union gunboats on the Tennessee River pound the Confederate lines, while some of Grant's 25,000 reinforcements arrive at Pittsburg Landing.

As this map (opposite, top) shows, the Battle of Shiloh took place on difficult terrain. Northern and Southern generals who had studied the tactics of European armies soon found that their tactics were unsuited to the rugged, heavily forested land of the American South.

Separated by only a few hundred yards, Union and Confederate infantry exchange fire (right), while cannonballs and exploding shells clip branches from the trees overhead. A Confederate soldier wrote of the first day at Shiloh: "Sharp, rending explosions and hurtling fragments made us shrink and cower . . . I marvelled how anyone could live under this raining death."

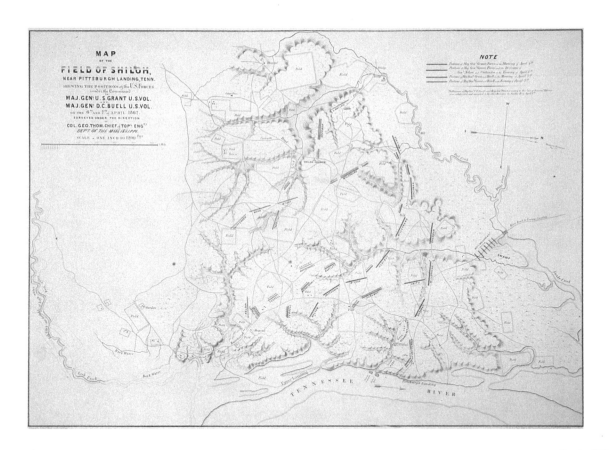

SHILOH: THE OUTCOME

The day ended with the conflict still undecided. As a cold rain fell, the exhausted soldiers of both sides dropped to sleep on the battlefield.

One of the casualties was the Confederate commander, Albert Sidney Johnston, mortally wounded while leading a charge on a Union-held peach orchard. Command passed to P.G.T. Beauregard. He was confident that his troops would drive Grant into the Tennessee River when the battle resumed in the morning.

But Union reinforcements had begun arriving at Pittsburg Landing late on April 6, and thousands of fresh troops poured in during the night. At 7 a.m., the fighting began again. This time, the Union troops did the attacking, supported by a massive artillery bombardment. Beauregard led several counterattacks, none successful. By four in the afternoon, the exhausted Confederates were in retreat back to Corinth.

The Battle of Shiloh (or the Battle of Pittsburg Landing, as the South called it) ended with the Union forces still in possession of the battlefield. In that sense, it was a Union victory. But the cost had been enormous. The Union had lost over 14,000 men—killed, wounded and missing—while the Confederates lost just under 11,000. More Americans fell at Shiloh than in all the Civil War's previous battles combined. The casualties shocked the public, both in the Union and in the Confederacy. Grant, formerly a hero, was labeled "the butcher" by Northern newspapers.

Drummer boys, some as young as nine years old, accompanied the Union and Confederate armies into battle. Shown here (above) is Johnny Clem, who won fame as the Union's "Drummer boy of Shiloh." Clem, promoted to sergeant after the Battle of Chickamauga in 1863, stayed in the army after the war and eventually retired as a general.

Like many Civil War battles and events, the Battle of Shiloh inspired music. This sheet-music cover (opposite, top) reflects American enthusiasm for the new art of photography; according to the publisher, the composer has "musically photographed" the brutal, two-day-long battle.

In this lithograph (right), Union reinforcements are shown racing into position at Shiloh. Shortly after arriving at the battlefield, Grant sent a message to General Lew Wallace, whose troops were slowly moving toward the fighting: "If you will get upon the field . . . it will be a move to our advantage, and possibly save the day to us. The rebel force is estimated at over 100,000 men."

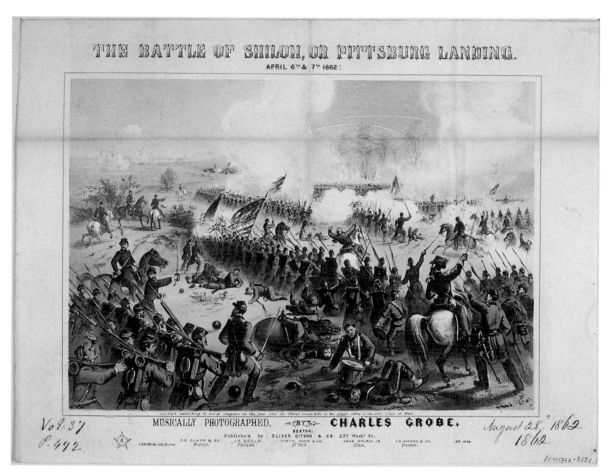

THE BATTLE OF SHILOH, OR PITTSBURG LANDING.

APRIL 6TH & 7TH 1862.

MUSICALLY PHOTOGRAPHED, BY CHARLES GROBE.

BOSTON:

Published by OLIVER DITSON & CO. 277 Wash" St.

C.C. CLAPP & CO. Boston. J.E. GOULD. Philada. FIRTH, POND & CO. N. York. JOHN CHURCH JR. Cin. J.C. HAYNES & CO. Boston.

THE BLOCKADE

On April 19, 1861, President Lincoln declared a blockade of all Confederate ports. The blockade's purpose was to keep Southern cotton and sugar from reaching Europe, and to prevent weapons and other supplies from reaching the Confederacy. The blockade did not alarm the Confederate government at first. President Davis had already forbidden exports of cotton, to force Britain and France—whose textile factories depended on Southern cotton—to intervene on the Confederacy's behalf. Also, blockading 3,500 miles of Southern coastline seemed an impossible task for the small Union Navy.

Under the able guidance of Navy Secretary Gideon Welles, however, the Union worked to put teeth in the blockade. The Union government bought hundreds of civilian vessels—including ferries and tugboats—and hastily converted them for blockade duty. The blockading ships cruised along the South's coasts on the Atlantic and the Gulf of Mexico, or took up stations outside key Southern ports. Smaller Union vessels patrolled the mouths of harbors. When an unidentified ship appeared, these "picket boats" fired rockets to signal the larger warships offshore to move in and catch the ship before it slipped out to sea or into the harbor.

Blockade duty was dull for the most part, until a blockade runner came into sight. These fast steamships carried cargoes between the Confederacy and ports in Bermuda and Cuba. By the end of 1861, the Union Navy managed to capture only about one out of every ten ships running the blockade.

The captured blockade runner Teaser *lies off Fortress Monroe, Virginia, in this photograph (above). By the time the* Teaser *was seized—in December 1864—only one out of every two runners made it through the Union blockade. Still, a blockade runner's owners could make a profit of several hundred percent from a single successful voyage, and blockade-running captains often received payments of $5,000 or more per trip.*

A Union sailor stands next to a naval gun mounted on the Teaser's *main deck. Most blockade runners, however, did not mount weapons, both to lighten the ship for speed and to make more space available for the guns, ammunition, medicine, and other goods so desperately needed by the Confederacy.*

NAVAL WAR

To strengthen the blockade, the Union Navy needed to seize harbors where its patrolling ships could stop for supplies and repairs. Only two Southern bases—Hampton Roads in Virginia, and Key West, Florida—were in Union hands at the outbreak of the war. Thus, blockading vessels spent almost as much time steaming to and from their bases as they did on patrol.

The Union's first move was to capture two Confederate forts on North Carolina's offshore islands. On August 28–29, 1861, a seven-ship Union fleet in Hatteras Inlet shelled the half-completed forts, while 900 soldiers and marines landed to occupy the islands.

A month later, Confederate forces abandoned Ship Island off Mississippi in the Gulf of Mexico. The capture of Ship Island gave the Union a base in the Gulf of Mexico and a staging point for the upcoming expedition against New Orleans. In November, a seventy-four-ship fleet under Captain Samuel Du Pont destroyed Confederate forts protecting Port Royal Sound, the body of water leading to Savannah, Georgia, and Charleston, South Carolina.

The Union's greatest naval triumph in the early part of the war came in February 1862, when an expedition under General Ambrose Burnside captured Roanoke Island off the coast of North Carolina. With the capture of Roanoke Island, the Union Navy now controlled Albemarle and Pamlico sounds, cutting North Carolina off from the Atlantic.

The seagoing counterpart of the army's drummer boys were the navy's "powder monkeys," young boys who brought powder charges to gun crews in action. This confident-looking powder monkey (right) was photographed aboard the Union warship New Hampshire off the South Carolina coast.

The Union Army and Navy often worked together in the Civil War. This engraving (below) shows Union infantry aboard landing barges in one of many amphibious landings along the coast of Virginia and the Carolinas. The Navy wanted to win bases for the Union's blockade squadrons.

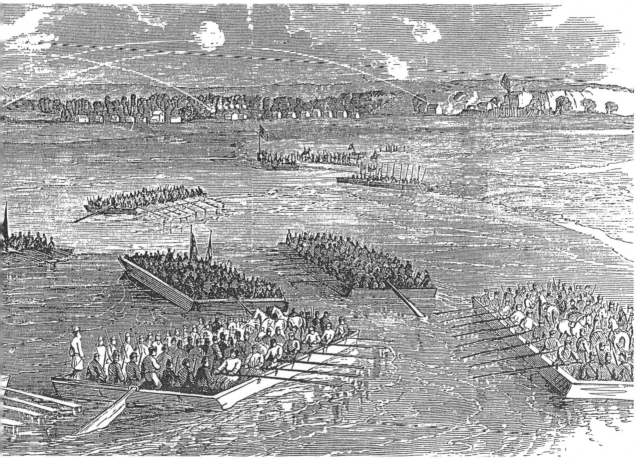

THE IRONCLADS

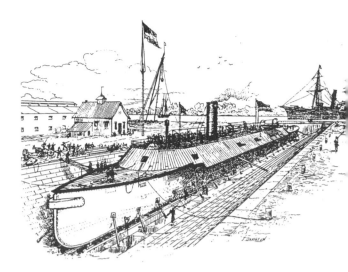

At the outbreak of war, the Union Navy consisted of only about forty ships and 25,000 sailors, most of them scattered in ports around the world. The small Union naval force had a big job: patrolling nearly 3,500 miles of Southern coastline to enforce the naval blockade proclaimed by President Lincoln. Also, shallow-draft gunboats were needed to support the army in its operations on the Mississippi and other inland waters. Lack of time and money led to improvisation; the gunboats that helped Grant capture forts Henry and Donelson, for example, were designed and built by an Indiana engineer, James B. Eads, with his own money.

Another naval innovator was Swedish-born John Ericsson. In early 1861, Ericsson offered the Union government plans for a new kind of warship—the ironclad. Instead of having a wooden hull, the new vessel would be plated with iron for protection from enemy cannonballs. Instead of conventional naval guns, which could fire in only one direction, the ironclad would have a revolving turret for its cannons. President Lincoln personally asked Ericsson to build an ironclad "for the destruction of the Rebel fleet." Spurred on by reports that the Confederacy was also working on an ironclad, Ericsson set up shop in the Brooklyn Navy Yard. Only 100 working days later, his creation, the *Monitor*, was ready for duty—not a day too soon. The Confederacy's ironclad, the *Merrimack* (called the *Virginia* by the Confederates), had already begun destroying the wooden warships of the Union Navy.

In April 1861, Union forces abandoned Gosport Navy Yard in Virginia, destroying its equipment and sinking the steam warship Merrimack *to keep it out of Confederate hands. Confederate engineers, however, raised the* Merrimack *and renamed it the* Virginia. *They covered the ship's sides with four-inch-thick iron plates to deflect shells, as shown in this engraving (above). Nine guns were mounted in an armored enclosure in its deck. The* Virginia *was launched on January 30, 1862, the same day as the Union ironclad* Monitor.

This set of engravings (opposite, top) depicts life on board the Union Navy's first and most famous ironclad, the Monitor. *Skeptical naval officers called the vessel "a tin can on a shingle." Some predicted that it wouldn't even float. The Navy Department's contract with Ericsson actually stated that he would have to refund the $275,000 cost of construction if the new-fangled warship wasn't a "complete success." Fortunately for both Ericsson and the Union, it was.*

Sailors aboard the Union ironclad Lehigh *run through gun drill—practicing loading and firing one of the ship's guns. The light cannon on wheels shown in this photograph (right) was an unusual weapon for an ironclad; most relied on heavier naval guns mounted in revolving turrets.*

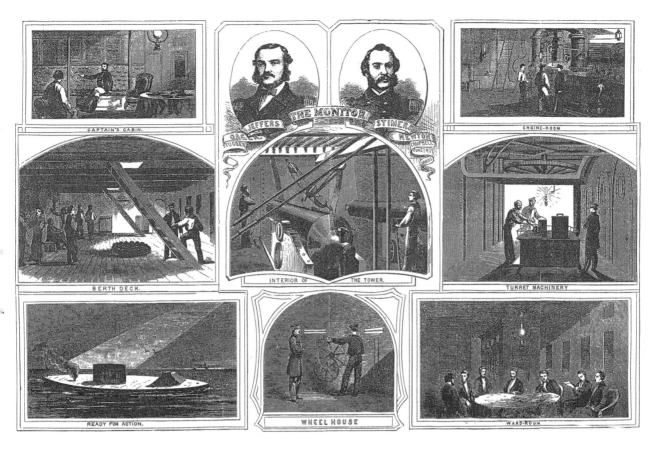

CAPTAIN'S CABIN.

THE MONITOR

GAC. JEFFERS — STIMERS NEWTON

ENGINE-ROOM

BERTH DECK.

INTERIOR OF THE TOWER.

TURRET MACHINERY

READY FOR ACTION.

WHEEL HOUSE

WARD-ROOM

THE *MONITOR* AND THE *MERRIMACK*

On March 8, 1862, the *Merrimack* steamed out of Norfolk, Virginia, to attack Union warships anchored offshore in Hampton Roads. Within a couple of hours, the *Merrimack* sank two Union vessels and forced a third aground. Shells from the Union ships bounced off the *Merrimack*'s sloping iron sides. The ironclad seemed unstoppable. Union leaders feared the *Merrimack* would steam up the Potomac River and attack Washington. But the Union's new ironclad, the *Monitor*, was already on its way to meet the Confederacy's naval threat. The *Monitor* arrived in Hampton Roads early on the morning of March 9, and the *Merrimack* steamed out to fight it.

The *Monitor* didn't seem to be a match for the *Merrimack*. The Union vessel was much smaller and mounted only two guns to the *Merrimack*'s nine. But the *Monitor*'s guns were in a revolving turret, while the *Merrimack*'s were fixed in rows along the ship's sides, so that only half could fire at one time. Also, the *Monitor*'s more powerful engine gave it an advantage in maneuvering.

For four hours, the two ironclads fired at each other. At times the warships were so close that their sides scraped. Finally, the battered *Merrimack* steamed away to the protection of Confederate shore batteries. Washington, and the rest of the Union's wooden navy, was safe—at least for the time being.

This lithograph shows clouds of gunpowder smoke surrounding the Monitor and the Merrimack as they pound away at each other at close range. After their engagement, the days of wooden warships were over forever. A newspaper in Britain, home of the world's mightiest fleet, stated that apart from two experimental ironclads, "There is not now a ship in the English navy . . . that it would not be madness to trust to an engagement with that little Monitor."

ISLAND NUMBER TEN

Union victories in the West continued after the fall of forts Henry and Donelson. Nashville, Tennessee, fell to Union general Don Carlos Buell on February 24, 1862. In early March, Confederate general Earl Van Dorn led a poorly equipped army of 12,000 men against Union general Samuel R. Curtis's forces at Pea Ridge, Arkansas. Van Dorn was defeated in the resulting battle, known as the Battle of Pea Ridge in the North and the Battle of Elkhorn Tavern in the South. The Union was winning its campaign to control the Mississippi River Valley.

But a big obstacle remained—Island Number Ten, a heavily-fortified island in a bend where the Mississippi flows from Missouri into Tennessee. Before his death at Shiloh, Albert Sidney Johnston had ordered General P.G.T. Beauregard to hold Island Number Ten and the nearby forts at New Madrid, Missouri, "at all costs."

A Union force under General John Pope, supported by a fleet under Commodore Andrew H. Foote, set out to clear the two positions. The forts at New Madrid fell in early March after a ten-day siege. To cut off Island Number Ten, the ironclad *Carondelet* made a daring nighttime run downriver past the fort's guns on April 4. Another gunboat followed two nights later. With protection from the two warships, the transports carrying Pope's troops made it safely downriver. Surrounded and under heavy bombardment, the island's commander, General W. W. Mackall, surrendered the 7,000-man garrison on April 7.

This series of wood-engravings (above) depicts scenes from the month-long Union campaign to capture Island Number Ten. Top: Commodore Foote's gunboats move downriver to scout Confederate positions. Center: Riverboats move armored barges with mounted guns (also known as mortar boats) into position. Bottom: The mortar boats bombard Confederate fortifications.

THE CAPTURE OF NEW ORLEANS

The fall of Island Number Ten sealed off one end of the Mississippi River. To win control of the other end, the Union had to take New Orleans, the South's gateway to the Gulf of Mexico.

Only a handful of Confederate troops and a few gunboats protected New Orleans. The city's main defenses, Fort Jackson and Fort St. Philip, were seventy-five miles downriver. Confederate leaders hoped that the guns of these forts, plus the Mississippi's swift current and sandbars, would keep the Union Navy away.

The Union assembled a forty-two-ship fleet in the Gulf of Mexico under the command of Flag Officer David Glasgow Farragut. In early April, Farragut's ships made it across the sandbars at the Mississippi's mouth. For a week, his gunboats fired 3,000 shells a day at forts Jackson and St. Philip. When the forts refused to surrender, Farragut decided to force his way past them. The risky move succeeded with the loss of only one Union vessel.

Once past the forts, the Union ships faced only the tiny gunboats of the Confederate "mosquito fleet," which they easily sank or drove off. On April 25, 1862, the citizens of New Orleans awoke to find Farragut's ships at anchor along the city's waterfront. Farragut waited three days for the city's surrender; when it didn't come, he sent marines ashore to raise the stars and stripes. A few days later, 15,000 Union troops under General Benjamin Butler landed to complete the conquest. The South's largest and wealthiest city was now in Union hands.

After taking New Orleans, Farragut's fleet moved upriver to capture Baton Rouge, Louisiana, and Natchez, Mississippi. The Union ships and 3,000 soldiers, however, failed to take the strategic river city of Vicksburg, Mississippi. This photograph (above) shows the Union fleet loading up with wood, coal, and other supplies before setting out for Vicksburg.

Flag officer Farragut's fleet makes its daring pre-dawn run past Fort Jackson and Fort St. Philip in this dramatic print (opposite, top). The combined firepower of the Union and Confederate guns on shore and on the river produced, in one historian's words, "the greatest fireworks display in American history."

A rebel tugboat pushed a flaming raft against the sides of Farragut's flagship, the Hartford, *but the Union vessel's crew got the fire under control and sank the tugboat. After that, Confederate gunboats tried to ram it, as shown in this print (right) from a painting by J. O. Davidson. The Hartford's powerful engines brought it to safety, but another Union vessel, the* Varuna, *was sunk.*

Part II
The End of the Beginning

The spring of 1862 was a hopeful time for the North. Victories in the West and at sea took some of the sting out of the defeat at Bull Run. The North planned to capture Richmond by way of an advance up the Virginia peninsula. But in April, when the Union Army was at the city's outskirts, a hard-hitting Confederate offensive led by Robert E. Lee drove them back. Meanwhile, Stonewall Jackson conducted a brilliant campaign in Virginia's Shenandoah Valley. Lee's chief fighting force, the Army of Northern Virginia, further humiliated the North by defeating Union forces near the old Bull Run battlefield in August.

Although the Union had superior numbers, the South had the superior military leadership of Lee and Jackson. Encouraged by victory on the peninsula and at Bull Run, Lee invaded Maryland in September. Union forces halted Lee at the Battle of Antietam—the bloodiest single day of the war. At the same time, in the West, another Confederate offensive sputtered out at the Battle of Perryville in Kentucky.

After the Union victory at Antietam, Abraham Lincoln issued a document that would change the course of the war—the Emancipation Proclamation, which declared all slaves in the Confederate states free as of January 1, 1863. The proclamation made the end of slavery, not just the defeat of the Confederacy, the Union's goal.

As 1862 ended, the Union was meeting with little success in the East. In December, Ambrose Burnside, the new commander of the Army of the Potomac, launched a fruitless and costly attack at Fredericksburg, Virginia. The only bright spot for the North was in the West, where the Union grip on the Mississippi continued to grow tighter.

In this lithograph, based on a painting by H. A. Ogden, Robert E. Lee and his staff watch the Union assault on Marye's Heights outside Fredericksburg, Virginia. "It is well that war is so terrible," Lee remarked sadly as the Union troops marched into heavy Confederate fire, "or we should grow too fond of it."

THE PENINSULAR CAMPAIGN

The Battle of Bull Run dashed Union hopes for a quick overland assault on Richmond, but both the press and the public in the North continued to call for the city's capture. In the spring of 1862, General George McClellan introduced a new plan. He wanted the Union Navy to land the Army of the Potomac on the peninsula of land between the York and James rivers in Virginia. From there, the plan was to move up the peninsula and take Richmond. McClellan believed this "Peninsular Campaign" would achieve victory with a minimum of Union casualties. Lincoln agreed to McClellan's proposal, but ordered that 40,000 troops be held back to defend Washington.

By early April, over 100,000 Union soldiers were on the tip of the peninsula, seventy miles from Richmond. The first obstacle was Yorktown. McClellan was convinced that the Confederates outnumbered his army. The general's intelligence adviser, detective Allan Pinkerton, greatly overestimated Confederate troop strength throughout the campaign. Also, the Confederate commander at Yorktown, General John B. Magruder, had his men make noise and march in circles to trick Union scouts into believing their numbers were larger.

After a month-long siege, General Magruder's troops slipped away and McClellan's men occupied Yorktown. McClellan's army and the retreating Confederates tangled at Williamsburg on May 5, but most of the Confederates had escaped the Union pursuit.

Rows of cannons and mortars stand at Camp Winfield Scott (right), the Army of the Potomac's base at Yorktown, Virginia. McClellan refused to advance until huge loads of equipment had arrived on the peninsula. According to his quartermaster's report, "Several thousand wagons, and the Richmond-York Railroad, were employed for land transportation; and steam vessels . . . almost without number, brought the supplies."

McClellan constantly wired Washington for more men as the Peninsular Campaign began: "Wagons and troops," began one message, "[are] absolutely necessary to enable me to advance to Richmond." In this drawing (below), Union troops march inland after landing from a fleet of transports in Hampton Roads.

FAIR OAKS AND SEVEN PINES

In the spring of 1862, McClellan crept slowly up the peninsula from Yorktown, blaming lack of reinforcements, bad weather, and poor maps for his slow progress toward Richmond. By the end of May, however, the Army of the Potomac was camped less than ten miles from Richmond, at a farm called Seven Pines.

But McClellan's army was in a dangerous position. Part of his force was stranded south of the rain-swollen Chickahominy River, exposed to attack and cut off from the rest of the army on the northern bank. On May 31, Confederate general Joseph E. Johnston struck at the Union forces south of the Chickahominy. The battle was fought over two days and in two places—at Seven Pines and at Fair Oaks. The Union force narrowly escaped disaster. If Johnston had been able to bring up reinforcements, he might have destroyed a large part of the Union Army. But the troops Johnston was counting on took the wrong road and arrived too late. Also, Union engineers threw bridges across the flooded Chickahominy, allowing fresh troops to cross the river and join the battle.

When the fighting ended on June 1, almost 6,000 Confederates had been killed or wounded, compared to about 4,500 for the Union. One of the Southern casualties was Joseph Johnston, who was too badly wounded to continue in command. Jefferson Davis replaced him with General Robert E. Lee—the man who would soon become the South's leading general.

The Army of the Potomac used balloons, shown in this photograph (right), to observe Confederate troop movements around Richmond and to direct artillery fire. At Fair Oaks, an observer wrote, "With the aid of good glasses [binoculars], we were enabled to view the whole affair between these powerful contending armies."

Like much popular Civil War artwork, this lithograph (below) of the Battle of Fair Oaks is inaccurate: Bayonet charges were a rare event, because the rifles used by both sides were hard-hitting and accurate. Virginia private Carlton McCarthy wrote that after a few battles, "The infantry found out that bayonets were not of much use, and did not hesitate to throw them away."

THE ARMY OF NORTHERN VIRGINIA

By April 1861, Robert E. Lee was a thirty-two-year veteran of the army. Union general in chief Winfield Scott thought so highly of Lee that he offered him command of the Union forces after the attack on Fort Sumter. Lee, who disliked slavery and secession, considered the offer, but finally decided that "save in defense of my native state, I never again desire to draw my sword." When Virginia seceded, however, he offered his services to the state.

Lee had little success in his first assignments—fighting the Union advance into western Virginia and strengthening Virginia's coastal defenses. But Jefferson Davis had confidence in Lee. In March 1862, Davis made him his chief military adviser. When General Joseph Johnston fell at Seven Pines, Davis made Lee commander of the Confederate army outside Richmond. Lee gave the force a new name: the Army of Northern Virginia.

Lee's "strong right arm" was General Thomas "Stonewall" Jackson. Like Lee, Jackson was a Virginian, a West Point graduate, and a Mexican War veteran. The resemblance ended there. Unlike the courtly, handsome Lee, Jackson was a tight-lipped, fanatically religious eccentric. Before the war, Jackson taught at the Virginia Military Institute, where his students nicknamed him "Tom Fool." But Jackson had proved his courage and leadership at Bull Run. Soon he would show that he was brilliant as well as brave.

Robert E. Lee (1807–70; above) was born into an aristocratic Virginia family. After graduating second in his class from West Point, he served on the frontier and in Mexico, where he was twice promoted for bravery. Lee was practically worshipped by the troops he commanded and the Southern civilians whose homes he protected. After meeting him, one Southern woman reportedly said, "I've heard of God, but I've seen General Lee."

Stonewall Jackson (right) rarely wore the splendid uniform shown in this postwar portrait. His usual dress consisted of an old coat (the same one he had worn in Mexico) and a cap with a cracked brim, but his seedy appearance camouflaged a brilliant military mind.

Arlington House was Lee's home until the beginning of the war. It was located across the Potomac River from Washington, D.C., on the Virginia side. The house and grounds were seized by Federal troops, shown in this photograph (below), in 1861, in a move to strengthen the areas around Washington. In 1865, Lee's former estate was converted into the Arlington National Cemetery.

Arlington House, June 28th 1864.

JACKSON'S VALLEY CAMPAIGN

Virginia's Shenandoah Valley, between the Blue Ridge and Allegheny mountain ranges, was an easy invasion route into Maryland. The Union Army needed to keep it out of Confederate hands in order to safeguard Washington. In the spring of 1862 there were about 65,000 Union troops in the valley, but many of these men, under Irvin McDowell, were to be sent to the peninsula as reinforcements.

The Confederates realized that the campaign to save Richmond might fail if these reinforcements reached McClellan. To pin down the Union troops, General Stonewall Jackson was ordered to lead 18,000 Confederates into the valley.

The Valley Campaign didn't begin well for Jackson. He made the mistake of attacking a large Union force under General Nathaniel Banks at Kernstown on March 23 and was driven back. But Jackson recovered quickly, moving west to strike at Union general John C. Frémont's army on May 8. For the next five weeks, Jackson went from victory to victory. His men moved swiftly, always appearing where Union commanders least expected them. In late May, Jackson attacked Union outposts at Front Royal, Strasburg, and Winchester. Alarmed and worried about Washington's safety, Lincoln canceled the transfer of McDowell's troops to the peninsula. After two more victories at Cross Keys and Port Republic, Jackson made a fighting retreat out of the valley and moved south to join Lee.

The high point of the Battle of Kernstown came when Union and Confederate regiments raced toward a stone wall crossing the battlefield, as depicted (right) by newspaper artist A. R. Waud. A Confederate participant wrote, "It was 'nip and tuck' which would reach it first; but the 37th [Virginia regiment] got there and, kneeling down, poured a deadly volley into the other at close quarters."

By June, Union forces had cut off all of Jackson's lines of retreat from the Shenandoah Valley, except for a gap between the towns of Strasburg and New Market. A Union force under General Charles Frémont tried to close the gap and capture Jackson and his men, but Jackson got through both towns safely. This engraving (below) shows Frémont's troops, weary after earlier fighting, on their march toward Strasburg.

Battle of Winchester
charge upon the rebels at the stone wall.

JEB STUART'S RIDE AROUND McCLELLAN

Lee had a plan to save Richmond and drive McClellan off the peninsula. He had already ordered a network of trenches to be dug around the city. Lee planned to use some of his force to guard these defenses and keep the Union troops out of Richmond. Then, gathering as many Southern troops as he could, he would trap McClellan on the banks of the Chickahominy River and destroy his army.

Before he could act, Lee needed to find out the strength and position of McClellan's forces. He gave the job to his cavalry commander, General James Ewell Brown ("Jeb") Stuart, a Virginian and, like Lee, a West Point graduate. Stuart was a showy soldier, fond of wearing a billowing gray cape and a broad-brimmed hat topped with an ostrich feather. Twenty-nine years old and eager for glory, Stuart was happy to accept the assignment.

On June 12, Stuart and 1,200 troopers left Richmond and rode east. Encountering only a few small Union patrols, Stuart quickly got the information Lee needed. Rather than return through the Union lines, Stuart decided to press on. The Confederate troopers improvised a bridge across the Chickahominy and raided around the edges of the Union Army's camps, capturing 170 prisoners and destroying wagon loads of supplies. By June 16, Stuart was back in Richmond. He and his troopers had covered 150 miles in four days and ridden completely around McClellan's army.

In this fanciful print, General Jeb Stuart (1833–64) issues orders to a Confederate cavalry scout during his celebrated "Ride around McClellan" on the peninsula. Smoke from a burning Union supply depot rises in the background. One of the cavalry commanders in McClellan's army was Philip St. George Cooke—Stuart's father-in-law. Stuart never forgave his relative for siding with the North, saying, "He will regret it but once—and that will be continuously."

THE BATTLE OF THE SEVEN DAYS

Robert E. Lee now had 85,000 troops under his command, including Stonewall Jackson's forces. On June 26, he began an offensive against the Army of the Potomac, with an attack on Union general Fitz-John Porter's corps at Mechanicsville, a town about ten miles northeast of Richmond. This assault began a week-long conflict known as the Battle of the Seven Days. Mechanicsville ended in a Confederate defeat when Jackson's troops failed to arrive at the battlefield on schedule. (Jackson fought poorly during the Battle of the Seven Days—possibly exhausted after his whirlwind campaign in the Shenandoah Valley.)

Undaunted, Lee attacked the next day at Gaines' Mill, several miles to the southeast. The Union troops put up a stiff fight, and Confederate casualties were heavy, but by the end of the day, Porter's troops were in retreat. McClellan, still convinced that his troops were outnumbered, ordered the entire army to withdraw to Harrison's Landing on the James River, despite protests by several of his generals.

Lee had saved Richmond. Now he had the chance to strike McClellan's huge, slow-moving army in its retreat. On June 29, Confederates attacked the Union Army at Savage's Station. But because of the enormity of the Union Army, Confederate officers became easily confused and most Union troops were able to escape. Lee, angry at the missed opportunities, snapped that McClellan "will get away because I cannot have my orders carried out."

A small division of regular soldiers served with the Army of the Potomac from 1862 to 1863. Because the experienced regulars were more reliable in combat than the volunteers, McClellan often used them in dangerous situations, such as providing covering fire for retreating troops. Here (above), the 5th Cavalry charges the Confederate lines at Gaines' Mill.

After the fighting at Savage's Station, the retreating Army of the Potomac had to leave behind a field hospital filled with 2,500 men—some wounded in battle and others wasted by disease. James F. Gibson took this photograph (right) of the abandoned soldiers.

MALVERN HILL

By July, McClellan's army had reached Harrison's Landing on the James River, where the exhausted Yankees could rest safely under the protection of Union gunboats. To block a possible Confederate attack on his new base, McClellan ordered fortifications built on 150-foot-high Malvern Hill.

Lee couldn't resist one more all-out attack on the Army of the Potomac. Despite McClellan's superior numbers and the strong defenses on Malvern Hill (including over 100 cannons), Lee ordered an assault. General James Longstreet had reported that Confederate artillery could overpower the Union guns. Lee also believed that the discouraged Union troops would flee rather than face a determined attack.

Both Longstreet and Lee were wrong. When Confederate artillery began shelling Malvern Hill on July 1, Union guns roared back, quickly putting the Confederate artillery out of action. Next, Lee's infantry charged up the hill—straight into determined Union rifle and artillery fire. Brigade after brigade was cut down. By the time Lee gave the order to abandon the assault, 5,500 Southerners lay dead or wounded on the slopes of Malvern Hill.

The Battle of Malvern Hill marked the end of the Peninsula Campaign. About 30,000 men on both sides had been killed, wounded, or captured— the Confederacy suffered higher casualties than the Union because of Lee's aggressive strategy. McClellan's bid to "take Richmond by the back door" had failed, but his army remained mostly intact. Lee wrote, "Under ordinary circumstances the federal army should have been destroyed."

This watercolor (right), from a sketch by Alfred Waud, shows a Confederate munitions train, on the verge of exploding, about to fall into Chickahominy Swamp after Union troops set fire to the railroad tracks. During their retreat to the James River, Union troops destroyed their own ammunition so it wouldn't fall into enemy hands.

Union troops stand fast against the Confederate assault on Malvern Hill in this Currier & Ives lithograph (below). Years later, former Confederate general D. H. Hill said of this battle, "It was not war, it was murder." After the battle, a Union officer reported that the thousands of wounded and dying Confederates gave the hill's slopes "a singular crawling effect."

Destruction of the locomotive on the bridge over the Rappahannock. A. R. Waud.

BACK TO AN OLD BATTLEFIELD

President Lincoln responded to the Union failure in the Peninsular Campaign by placing all the Union forces in Virginia (except McClellan's Army of the Potomac) under the command of General John Pope.

Pope was a very different officer from the cautious, methodical McClellan. The hero of the capture of Island Number Ten, Pope had a reputation as a fighting general. He liked to say that he had his "headquarters in the saddle." Robert E. Lee, angered at Pope's harsh treatment of Confederate civilians in Union-occupied Virginia, said that Pope had his "headquarters where his hindquarters ought to be."

On August 9, Stonewall Jackson attacked the advance guard of Pope's army at Cedar Mountain, Virginia. The Union forces, led by General Nathaniel Banks, almost defeated Jackson, but a Confederate division under General A. P. Hill joined the fight, allowing Jackson to withdraw and join forces with Lee.

Pope and Lee maneuvered against each other until Jeb Stuart's cavalry raided Pope's camp and seized a telegram stating that reinforcements were on their way to the Union force. Deciding to strike Pope before the reinforcements arrived, Lee sent Stonewall Jackson to move behind the Union Army and cut it off from Washington. Jackson's soldiers quickly captured Pope's main supply depot at Manassas Junction. After destroying whatever they couldn't eat or carry, Jackson's men dug in along a ridge near the old battlefield at Bull Run.

This illustration (above) shows General Lee and his staff watching their troops in action at the Second Battle of Bull Run. The soft-spoken Lee found it hard to refer to the Northern soldiers as "the enemy"—instead, he usually called them "those people."

On a hot summer day in August 1862, children in this photograph (right) watch as Union cavalrymen pause to water their horses in Bull Run, the slow-moving stream near which two of the Civil War's greatest battles were fought.

SECOND BULL RUN

Lee's plan was to wait for Pope to attack Stonewall Jackson's force near Bull Run. While Jackson kept Pope busy, General James Longstreet's forces would strike at Pope's left flank.

Pope launched his assault on Jackson's positions on August 29, but Lee and Longstreet failed to agree on the timing of Longstreet's attack. Pope was able to hammer at Jackson throughout the day. Believing the Confederates were about to withdraw, Pope telegraphed Lincoln announcing a Union victory.

When the Union troops renewed their attack in the morning, however, they found Jackson's forces still in position—with Longstreet's forces adding to his strength. Fierce fighting continued all day, with some Confederate units running so low on ammunition that they hurled rocks at the attacking Yankees. But the rebels steadily pushed the Union troops back. By nightfall, the Union forces were in retreat.

The Second Battle of Bull Run (or the Battle of Second Manassas, as Southerners called it) was, like the first, a Union defeat. Pope's army had suffered about 16,000 casualties compared to Lee's 10,000, and almost all of Virginia was back under Confederate control.

Lincoln decided to combine Pope's forces with McClellan's, saying, "If he [McClellan] can't fight himself, he excels in making others ready to fight." McClellan greeted the weary troops on September 2, as they slogged back to Washington.

Newspaper artist A. R. Waud drew this eyewitness sketch (right) of Union troops fleeing the battlefield at Bull Run. A Confederate private wrote at the battle's end, "Directly in front of our position, the whole plain, as far as the eye can reach, is covered with the blue of the enemy—some brigades flying in disorder . . . "

With his troops close to the breaking point, Stonewall Jackson called on General James Longstreet for help during the second day of fighting at Bull Run. Rather than attack Pope's 32,000 men head-on, Longstreet brought up his artillery and battered the Union troops, as shown in this photograph (below), before sending his infantry into battle.

LEE ADVANCES NORTH

After their victory at Second Bull Run, Robert E. Lee and Jefferson Davis decided that the best way to defend the Confederacy was to invade the North. If the South advanced into Maryland and perhaps also into Pennsylvania, Union troops would have to withdraw from Virginia to deal with the invaders. The Union government might be persuaded to accept the Confederacy's independence.

On September 5, 1862, Lee's 40,000-strong army began crossing the Potomac River into Maryland. By the time McClellan moved to stop him—with a force of 88,000 men—Lee had already vanished into the mountainous region of western Maryland.

On September 13, the Union had an incredible stroke of good luck. Three Union soldiers found a carelessly discarded copy of Lee's battle plan. The paper revealed that Lee had split his army into four separate forces and gave the position of each one. McClellan had the information he needed to defeat Lee completely—but he didn't move quickly enough. News of the find leaked out and reached Lee, who quickly changed his plans. By the time McClellan moved, Stonewall Jackson had already carried out one of Lee's goals—the capture of the huge Union supply depot at Harpers Ferry, Virginia. The base was taken, along with 12,000 prisoners, on September 15.

Meanwhile, Lee's scattered forces pulled together and moved toward McClellan, who had arrived at Antietam Creek near the town of Sharpsburg, Maryland.

Alexander Gardner took this photograph (right) of Sharpsburg's main street shortly before the Battle of Antietam. This quiet Maryland town was ill-prepared for the thousands of wounded and dying soldiers who would fill its houses and churches once the battle was over.

As the sun sets, Union scouts, shown in the lower left of this watercolor after a drawing by A. R. Waud (below), watch as the Army of Northern Virginia crosses the Potomac River at White's Ford, Virginia. A Confederate cavalryman later wrote, "There were few moments, perhaps, from the beginning to the close of the war, of excitement more intense . . . than when we ascended the opposite bank," into Maryland.

ANTIETAM

On September 17, the Army of the Potomac attacked Lee's forces near Sharpsburg, beginning what was called the Battle of Antietam in the North and the Battle of Sharpsburg in the South. If McClellan had attacked on the 16th, he might have quickly overwhelmed the Confederates, who were greatly outnumbered. During the night of the 16th, however, Stonewall Jackson and his men had arrived to reinforce Lee.

Once again McClellan believed—incorrectly—that his army was outnumbered. So, instead of ordering one major coordinated assault, McClellan had his generals make several disjointed attacks on different parts of Lee's force. As a result, the Battle of Antietam turned into a series of savage close-range fights. A Union officer later recalled his men "loading and firing with demoniacal fury and laughing and shouting hysterically" at Confederates only a few yards away. Bullets and shells flew so thick and fast that some units were practically wiped out. One Texas regiment had 82 percent of its officers and troops killed in a few hours.

The tide of battle began to turn in the late afternoon, when Union general Ambrose Burnside managed to get his troops across a stone bridge over Antietam Creek. Lee's army was now in danger of complete destruction. Suddenly, a new Confederate force arrived on the battlefield; it was A. P. Hill's division from Harpers Ferry. With Hill's arrival, General McClellan decided not to send his last reserves into the fight, and the Battle of Antietam was over.

This sketch (above) by Edwin Forbes shows troops of General Ambrose Burnside's corps charging across the stone bridge spanning Antietam Creek. Burnside's first two attempts to take the bridge failed with heavy casualties. Antietam Creek was shallow and could have been safely forded out of range of Confederate snipers, but Burnside hadn't bothered to check its depth.

A Union officer prepared this detailed map (opposite, top) of the battleground of Antietam, showing the positions of Union and Confederate forces on the bloody Sunday of September 17, 1862. Sharpsburg, Maryland, is at lower left; Antietam Creek runs through the right portion of the map.

Urged on by officers with swords drawn, Union troops move into action at Antietam (right). The building in the background is the Dunker Church, meeting place of a German pacifist (antiwar) religious group. It was the scene of some of the heaviest fighting of the battle.

ANTIETAM: THE AFTERMATH

At dawn on September 18, 1862, Lee had fewer than 30,000 men who were still able to fight. But McClellan decided not to renew the battle—even though Lincoln had ordered him to destroy Lee's army if he had the chance. On the night of the 18th, Lee retreated into the safety of the Shenandoah Valley. On September 20, McClellan telegraphed Lincoln, "Maryland is entirely freed from the presence of the enemy, who has been driven across the Potomac. No fears need now be entertained for the safety of Pennsylvania."

Lee, a "born gambler" in one historian's words, had gambled and lost. The Confederacy's first invasion of the North had been halted and turned back with heavy casualties.

Antietam was a Union victory, but the cost was enormous. Six thousand soldiers had been killed and 17,000 more wounded, with the Union suffering about twenty-five percent higher casualties than the Confederates. September 17, 1862, was the single bloodiest day in American military history. Combat deaths at Antietam—a single battle—were more than twice those of all previous American wars combined.

The First Battle of Bull Run had shown both North and South that the war would not be a short one. Shiloh had proved to both sides that the war would be bloody. But not until Antietam did the Union and the Confederacy realize just how brutal and costly the war had become—and the end was nowhere in sight.

Photographs from the Antietam battlefield showed the American public its first views of the horrifying casualties of large-scale warfare. Alexander Gardner took this picture (above) of dead Confederate artillerymen near the Dunker Church (seen in the background) after the battle was over.

The bodies of Confederate soldiers lie in heaps along "Bloody Lane," southeast of Dunker Church, in this photograph. They had at first taken refuge in this sunken farm road. But Union troops broke through the center of the Confederate line, pouring rifle fire into the road from above. In the words of a Northern reporter, "The Confederates had gone down as the grass falls before the scythe."

THE WAR IN THE WEST

Robert E. Lee's invasion of Maryland was one half of a double offensive planned by Lee and Davis. The second half took place in the West, where General Braxton Bragg had taken command of Confederate forces. Bragg was to move into Kentucky from Tennessee and, if possible, to invade Ohio and Indiana.

Bragg's army left Chattanooga and advanced toward Louisville, Kentucky, in late August. The commander of the Union Army in Ohio, General Don Carlos Buell, moved to stop him. They met in battle at Perryville, Kentucky, on October 8. The Battle of Perryville ended in a Union victory, but Bragg withdrew to safety in Tennessee.

Perryville was one of a series of Confederate defeats in the West in 1862. In May, Ulysses S. Grant had captured Corinth, Mississippi. Two months later, he had been promoted to commander of the Army of the Tennessee, leaving General William S. Rosecrans in charge at Corinth. In October, Rosecrans successfully defended the city against a Confederate attack.

The Union's grip on the Mississippi River, though tightening, was not yet complete. Baton Rouge, Louisiana, and Natchez, Mississippi, fell to Union gunboats in May. Memphis was captured in June after a naval battle. But as 1862 ended, two major Mississippi River ports—Vicksburg, Mississippi, and Port Hudson, Louisiana— remained in Confederate hands. The capture of these two cities was now the Union's major goal in the West.

Braxton Bragg (left) treated his troops harshly, both as a Confederate general and as a young officer in the Mexican War. (His men tried to kill him by exploding a shell under his bed.) Bragg often seemed to lose his nerve when he was on the brink of victory. Fellow generals urged Jefferson Davis to dismiss him, but the Confederate president, a friend of Bragg's, kept him in command in the West until December 1863.

The Union Army in the West was about as large as the Army of the Potomac when it set out to capture Corinth, Mississippi, in April 1862. The slow-moving army—shown here (below) on the march through swampy terrain—finally reached Corinth in late May. Confederate forces under P.G.T. Beauregard, outnumbered by more than two to one, evacuated the city after minor skirmishing.

A UNION CHANGE IN COMMAND

In autumn 1862, Abraham Lincoln still hadn't found a general who would bring the Union victory in the East. He had such a soldier in the West—General Ulysses S. Grant. After Shiloh, some congressmen had urged Lincoln to dismiss Grant, claiming that Grant's incompetence had led to the Union's heavy casualties. Some accused Grant of being drunk during the fighting. Lincoln had refused to relieve Grant of command, stating, "I cannot spare this man—he fights."

But a fighting general to lead the Army of the Potomac proved hard to find. Irvin McDowell had failed, then George McClellan, then John Pope. Given a second chance, McClellan had managed to stop Lee at Antietam, but lost his opportunity to destroy Lee's army. On October 6, General Henry W. Halleck, general in chief of all of the Union armies, ordered McClellan to cross the Potomac and attack the Army of Northern Virginia. But as he had done on the peninsula and at Antietam, McClellan hesitated. While the Union general delayed, Jeb Stuart's cavalry rode once again around the Army of the Potomac. By the time the Union Army crossed the Potomac on November 6, any hope of a surprise attack on Lee was gone.

Fed up, Lincoln relieved McClellan of his post, this time for good. Command of the Army of the Potomac passed to General Ambrose Burnside. Burnside believed he was unfit for the job and begged that command be given to someone else, but Halleck and Lincoln refused to reconsider.

Like many generals on both sides, Ambrose Burnside (1824–81; above) was a graduate of West Point and a Mexican War veteran. After the Mexican War, he had left the army and gone broke designing and manufacturing a new kind of rifle. In 1858, his friend George McClellan gave him a job and assisted him out of debt. Burnside was well known for his extravagant whiskers, which became known as "sideburns."

Lincoln's disappointment in McClellan became well known after the Union commander's retreat on the peninsula in the summer of 1862. This Northern cartoon (opposite, top) shows McClellan "in hot water" as the president examines his "poor feet"—which the cartoonist implies were made sore by running away from the enemy.

On October 1, 1862, President Lincoln (right, in top hat) traveled to McClellan's headquarters at Harpers Ferry, Virginia, to prod the general (sixth from the left) into action. Photographer Alexander Gardner was on hand to record the scene.

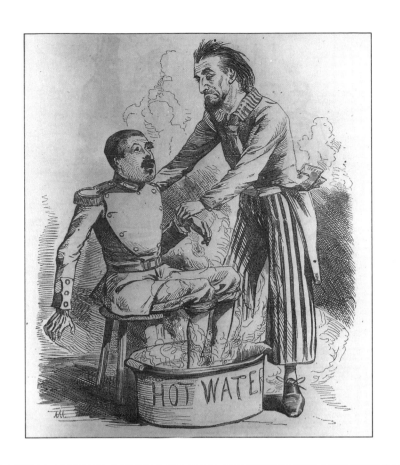

FREDERICKSBURG

Burnside formally replaced McClellan on November 7, 1862. Within a week, he had presented Lincoln with a plan to capture Confederate-held Fredericksburg along the Rappahannock River in Virginia. Lincoln agreed to Burnside's proposal.

To move the Army of the Potomac across the Rappahannock, Burnside needed to build a pontoon bridge across the river. The pontoons arrived far behind schedule. By the time the Union troops began to cross, Lee was well aware of Burnside's plan. He abandoned Fredericksburg and ordered his 80,000 Confederates to dig in on Marye's Heights, a high ridge overlooking the town.

The Army of the Potomac finally crossed into Fredericksburg on December 12. Burnside decided to attack Marye's Heights in a direct assault. On the foggy morning of December 13, the first of 60,000 Union troops charged a stone wall at the base of the heights.

From their well-protected trenches, the Confederates let loose a hail of bullets and cannonballs. Burnside ordered charge after charge up Marye's Heights. All failed. By the end of the day, thousands of Union troops lay dead or wounded in front of the Confederate trenches.

The next morning, Burnside himself prepared to lead another charge, but his officers talked him out of it. Fredericksburg was a disaster for the Union. The Army of the Potomac had lost 12,000 men with nothing to show for their heroic sacrifice. There would be no more fighting in Virginia until spring of the next year.

This color lithograph shows Union engineers building the pontoon bridge across the icy Rappahannock River. While they worked, Confederate snipers hidden in Fredericksburg kept up steady, harassing fire. As shown at upper right, a Michigan regiment had to paddle across the 400-foot-wide river, using pontoons as assault boats, to silence the snipers.

Resource Guide

Key to picture positions: (T) top, (C) center, (B) bottom; and in combinations: (TL) top left, (TR) top right, (BL) bottom left, (BR) bottom right, (RC) right center, (LC) left center.

Key to picture locations within the Library of Congress collections (and where available, photo negative numbers): P - Prints and Photographs Division; R - Rare Book Division; G - General Collections; MSS - Manuscript Division; G&M - Geography Division

PICTURES IN THIS VOLUME

2–3 Camp Davies, P **4–5** family, P **6–7** music cover, P **8–9** map, G

Timeline: **10–11** TL, troops, P, B8184-10076; BR, Bull Run, G **12–13** TL, Benjamin, P, USZ62-13690; BL, Roanoke Island, P; TR, broadside, P, USZ62-39368 **14–15** TL, Little Crow, P, USZ61-83; TR, Chase, P, USZ62-5761; BR, Fredericksburg, P, USZ62-7001

Part I: **16–17** flag, P **18–19** TL, newspaper, G; TR, Anderson, G; BL, Sumter, P **20–21** TR, portraits, P; C, tobacco labels, R **22–23** TL, uniforms, P; TR, camp, P, B8184-10016; BR, generals, P **24–25** TL, Capitol, P, USA7-5062; TR, guards, P, B8171-290; BR, map, P **26–27** TL, Ruffin, P, USZ62-11614; C, map, P **28–29** TL, Davis, G; TR, house, P, B8171-3376; BR, aerial view, P **30–31** C, cartoon, P **32–33** TL, Magruder, G; TR, mountain, P, USZ62-14034; BR, Big Bethel, P, USZ62-31755 **34–35** TR, Lyon, P; C, Wilson's Creek, P, USZ62-42579 **36–37** TL, map, P; TR, battle, P; BR, oxen, P, USZ62-13947 **38–39** TL, Jackson, G; TR, music cover, P; TR, troops, P, B8184-10006 **40–41** TR, McClellan, P; C, army, P, USZC4-1033 **42–43** TL, Mason, G; BL, Slidell, G; BR, *Trent*, USZ62-17253 **44–45** TL, Halleck, G; TR, gunboats, P, USZ62-16826; BR, Fort Donelson, P, USZ62-17152 **46–47** TL, map, P; TR, infantry, P,

USZC4-1910; BR, boats, R **48–49** TL, drummer boy, P, USZ62-11596; TR, music cover, P; BR, land battle, P, USZ62-3579 **50–51** C, *Teaser*, P, B8171-7414; BR, cannon, P, B811-482 **52–53** TR, powder monkey, P, B8171-4016; C, boats, G **54–55** TL, *Virginia*, G; TR, *Monitor*, P; BR, gun drill, P, B8184-B686 **56–57** battle, P **58–59** TL, scenes, P; BR, boats, P **60–61** TL, loading, P, B8184-10645; TR, forts, P; BR, *Hartford*, P

Part II: **62–63** Lee and staff, P **64–65** TR, Yorktown, P, B8171-2358; C, peninsula, P, USZ62-4281 **66–67** TR, balloon, P, B8171-2348; C, battle, P **68–69** TL, Lee, G; TR, Jackson, P; BR, house, P, B8184-10262 **70–71** TR, Kernstown, P, USZ62-7003; C, Frémont's troops, P, USZ62-33452 **72–73** Stuart, P, USZ62-5109 **74–75** TR, horses, P, USZ62-11628; wounded soldiers, P, B8171-491 **76–77** TR, train, P; C, battle, P **78–79** C, battle, P, USZ62-19887; BR, children, P, B8171-313 **80–81** TR, fleeing, P; C, Longstreet's troops, P, USZ62-19890 **82–83** TR, Sharpsburg, P, B8171-599; C, river, P **84–85** TL, bridge, P, USZ62-79225; TR, map, P; BR, battle, P **86–87** TL, Dunker Church, P; BR, Bloody Lane, P, B8171-553 **88–89** TR, Bragg, G; C, battle, R **90–91** TL, Burnside, P; TR, cartoon, P, USZ62-32540; BR, Lincoln and men, P **92–93** battle, P, USZC4-1579

SUGGESTED READING

BATTY, PETER AND PETER PARISH. *The Divided Union.* Topsfield, MA: Salem House, 1987.

CATTON, BRUCE. *The American Heritage Picture History of the Civil War.* New York: Bonanza Books, 1982.

FOMER, ERIC AND OLIVIA MAHONEY. *A House Divided.* Chicago: Chicago Historical Society, 1990.

SMITH, CARTER. *The Civil War.* New York: Facts on File, 1989.

TIME-LIFE. *Brother Against Brother.* New York: Prentice Hall, 1990.

Index

Page numbers in *italics* indicate illustrations